LIFE ISSUES

RUNNING AWAY

David K. Fremon

BENCHMARK BOOKS

MARSHALL CAVENDISH

NEW YORK

23

Marshall Cavendish Corporation
s Road
10591

l Cavendish Corporation

Library of Congress Cataloging-in-Publication Data

Fremon, David.
    Running away / by David Fremon.
        p.   cm. — (Life issues)
    Includes bibliographical references and index.
    ISBN 0-7614-0019-2 (lib. bdg.)
    1. Runaway teenagers—United States—Juvenile literature.
    I. Title. II. Series.
    HV1431.F74 1996
    362.7'4—dc20   95-11185
                                              CIP
                                              AC

4/96

Printed and bound in the United States of America

Produced by Jacquerie Productions

Photographic Note
Several persons depicted in this book are photographic models; their appearance in these photographs is solely to
dramatize some of the situations and choices facing readers of the Life Issues series.

Photo Credits
Boys Town: p. 42, 80
Covenant House: p. 4; 54; 71, 86 (George Wirt)
Richard B. Levine: p. 6,
Impact Visuals: p. 16, 58 (Donna DeCesare); 18 (Catherine Smith); 25 (Adam Taylor); 26 (Dana Schuerholz);
        28, 36 (Andrew Lichtenstein); 57 (Jim Tynan); 61 (Gabe Kirchheimer); 67 (Jim West); 76 (Lisa Terry);
        82 (Dan Habib)
Ed Kashi: p. 85
The Picture Cube: p. 9 (Huntly Hersch); 14 (Tom McCarthy Photos); 21, 89 (Jeff Greenberg); 22 (Dennis MacDonald);
        32 (W.B. Spunbarg); 39 (George Goodwin); 50 (Henryk T. Kaiser); 62 (Nancy Sheehan); 64 (Larry Lawfer),
        68 (D&I MacDonald); 79 (E. Williamson)
Frances M. Roberts: p. 47, 72
Swanstock: p. 34 (David H. Wells)

Cover photo: The Picture Cube (Cleo)

The producer would like to thank Jacqueline Callahan-Stewart for reviewing this manuscript.

To Karl

CONTENTS

Prologue

Almost everyone at one time or another has thought about running away from home. School seems too rough, or your family gets on your nerves, or the world just seems like it might be more exciting in a big city or another state. Often, the would-be runaway makes plans: I'll get up early tomorrow and catch the next bus out of town. But then the new day dawns, the irritation has passed, and home isn't such a bad place after all.

Every year, thousands of young people decide that home or school really is a bad place, and they follow through on their plans to run away. Some feel that they are no longer safe at home. They choose the unknown risks of street life over the known dangers of domestic violence or sexual abuse. Others are forced out of their homes by their families. Some runaways leave because they are in trouble and are afraid to confront their parents with the problem. Others find that school is the problem: they face failure in classes, taunts from unfriendly classmates, or the terror of gangs. Still others simply feel misunderstood or unloved, and feel there is no reason to stay. For runaways, it seems the only way out is just that—out of school, out of the home, and out of town.

No one can truthfully promise a troubled teen that staying home will make everything work out in the end. For some, everything will not be all right. In fact, everything could get a lot worse. In extreme cases, leaving home may not just be a logical solution, it may the sanest solution.

Even so, too many young people leave home without giving thought to what lies ahead of them. Once they reach the outside world, they find it can be indifferent to outright hostile. The "friends" they encounter may be friends only until they can grab the runaway's money or possessions. A life of sex, drugs, and alcohol may seem like fun at first, but it can quickly degenerate into poor health or even death.

Life on the streets is no game—it can be deadly serious. Few teenagers are prepared to make the decisions that will lead safely to a real future. This book looks at the reasons for running away and what a runaway can expect to encounter. It discusses alternatives to running away, and it tells you how to get assistance from the many agencies that help teenagers. It also examines what may be the most difficult part of the runaway process—returning home.

If you are looking at this book, you may be considering running away or you may know someone who is planning a run. Before you or your friend goes, know the very real dangers and consider the alternatives.

1

WHO RUNS AWAY?

*Tom's mind was made up now. He was gloomy and desperate.
He was a forsaken, friendless boy, he said; nobody
loved him; when they found out what they'd driven him to,
perhaps they would be sorry.*
—Mark Twain, *The Adventures of Tom Sawyer*

Every Friday night, hundreds of teenagers congregate near the corner of Clark and Belmont in Chicago's Lake View neighborhood. A donut shop there is a landmark—known nationwide—for young people. Word passes through underground networks, "If you're going to Chicago, start at the corner of Clark and Belmont."

The arcades, pawnshops, single-room hotels, army surplus stores, tattoo parlors, and coffee houses attract a fascinating mix of young people. Who gathers here? Some may be skinheads looking for a fight. Others are gang members. Many are tourists from the suburbs, drawn by the action and the chance to meet other teens. Some are neighborhood people on their way home.

And some are runaways. Of these, many are away from home for a day or two, giving both themselves and their parents a chance to cool off after an argument. Others are on the street for the longer term, their chances for a safe return home virtually zero.

Passersby may encounter a sea of humanity—the skinheads with shaved heads, punks with pink

Most young people go to school, hang out with their friends, and go home to their families every day. For many runaway teens, school is a distant memory and home is an abandoned building or an alley.

Mohawk haircuts and black motorcycle jackets, kids with multiple earrings, nose rings, tongue rings or belly-button rings, and many dressed in more convention- al styles. Looks may be deceiving. The young woman with the tattoo and nose ring may be working downtown and earning a $30,000 annual salary. The in-line skater wearing a Walkman who just zoomed by may run his own business. All the people here dress and act any way they want. It's a perfect place for a run- away to blend into a crowd and avoid detection.

Some of these Friday night celebrants will go home to good jobs or fami- lies in the suburbs. Many of the runaways will go "home" to abandoned apart- ments or alleys. For some, the space they currently occupy is the closest thing to home that they can claim.

If suburban kids talk about malls and sports and schools while visiting Lake View, other kids have different stories. Andi, a 16-year-old, is an example.

"I had home problems," she related. "My grandmother, who was an alco- holic, beat me. My father molested me nonstop for years. I was afraid to tell any- one about it. Finally, I just left.

"When I came here, to Chicago, I was lucky because I'm cute. A lot of johns [customers of prostitutes] like cute young girls. Prostitution is how I got my drugs. I'd take almost almost anything. I'd even do cough syrup to get high."

Andi continued, "One time, I was scoring some drugs in an alley down by Cabrini-Green [a low-income housing project]. I got jumped and got pregnant and had to get an abortion."

"I went into a hospital, Chicago Mental Hospital, for a six-month detox program. As soon as I got out of there, I ran away again," she continued. "Then I was working. One night, walking in Uptown, I got mugged. I used that as an excuse to quit working. I hung out here for two months. During that time, I went to a dentist. He must have called my mom. They caught me and put me in the mental hospital for another three months. By this time my father was in the men- tal ward of a hospital, diagnosed as a schizophrenic."

Andi's story reveals more perils than are found in the lifetimes of most people twice her age. Some of her account might be exaggerated; runaways are often known to give different names and life stories at each telling. But the hor- rors she describes—abuse at home, prostitution, drugs, rape, pregnancy, deten- tion in correctional centers or mental hospitals—are very real. They are hazards many runaways encounter sooner or later.

Dan, an 18-year-old, told a different tale. "I've been on the streets for a year and a half," he said. "I'm bisexual. My father kicked me out of the house when he found out I'm gay. Sometime when I was gone my father moved. I don't know where he is anymore."

The father in Dan's life has been replaced by a series of "sugar daddies," older men who let him live with them in exchange for sex. "I've had about twen- ty sugar daddies. I tend to move on and blow them off after a bit." Dan's current

Sex, drugs, and alcohol are often at the center of life as a runaway. It's a dangerous and very unhealthy way to live.

sugar daddy is a good one, he said. "He got me a job as a home-health care worker, babysitting old men." But Dan, who said he wanted to become a computer programmer, did not know whether he would stay with this provider for long.

"So far, Dan's led a charmed life," said Rev. Lee Lowrey of the Night Ministry, a group that tends to the needs of street people. "But that lucky spell could snap at any time. If Dan's not careful, he may run into a sugar daddy who doesn't take kindly to the thought of Dan leaving him, and Dan may wind up as a statistic in the morgue."

A young California woman named Maria was not so lucky. Maria was a chronic runaway in the early 1980s. She skipped home so many times that her parents no longer bothered to report her runs to the police. One night a stranger picked her up as she was hitchhiking. The man took her off the road, raped her, chopped off her arms with an ax, and abandoned her. Somehow, she managed to return to the road and notify the police.

RUNAWAYS IN HISTORY

Tales of runaways abound in American history. The hope of adventure beyond the horizon has always lured youngsters. For many, running off to sea, to join the circus, or to hunt buffalo on the frontier seemed much more attractive than toiling on their parents' farm.

But for most of the country's history, laws made by adults curbed the rights of young people. One example was a 1642 Connecticut law which forbade in children "any stubborn or rebellious carriage against their parents."

Famed frontiersman Kit Carson was one such youthful runaway. After his father died, his stepfather sent him off to be an apprentice to saddle maker David Workman. But tales of excitement lured him west. One night he found a mule and rode off to join a westbound wagon train.

Literature also abounds with tales of those who fled from home. Mark Twain's Tom Sawyer left an unappreciative Aunt Polly but returned in time to attend his own funeral. Toby Tyler fled stern Uncle Daniel to join the circus.

In reality, early American society did not treat runaways favorably. Most Americans lived on small farms, and children were considered a resource. A child who ran away left one less person to help with the work. Flight from the family was considered a sin, not a lifestyle choice. Captured runaways were often thrown into almshouses with the poor and the ill. Those who ran away from families in the cities were often sent to work on western farms.

Attitudes changed only slightly in the late nineteenth century. Many young people went to northeastern cities in search of work. They found jobs requiring long hours for little money in unsafe sweatshops. Some employers even forced the young workers to be chained to their work stations.

Runaways were considered to be in need of help. They were considered mentally unbalanced or emotional weaklings. Most ended up in newly created "schools of reform," which were little more than prisons for young people.

During the Great Depression of the 1930s, thousands of young people left home. They were not adventure seekers or people unhappy with home life. They, like their parents, were victims of the nation's widespread poverty and unemployment.

These Depression runaways often left home so that their parents would have one less mouth to feed. Most hoped to find a job somewhere and eventually return to share their good fortune with their family. Older boys were the first to leave home. Younger brothers followed. These young travelers thumbed from town to town or hopped boxcars. At night, they stayed in hobo jungles with older wanderers. Girls followed. A runaway girl usually coupled with a boy as cook, housekeeper, and sex partner.

The towns they traveled to usually offered no more work than the towns they left. Likewise, they seldom offered hospitality. Young people found within town limits were often given twenty-four hours to leave. If the local police were generous, they drove the young people to the county line before ordering them away.

During World War II, runaways were not a major problem. Young people who wanted to leave home joined the army or found a defense-related job. After the war, the relative prosperity of the country helped keep the runaway numbers low. But the rising divorce rate and the breakdown of the extended family caused problems that would lead to a rise in the runaway rate.

"Baby boomers," children born after the end of World War II, swelled the adolescent population in the 1960s. At the same time, the number of jobs and services available to them decreased. Families moved frequently. This high mobility led to lack of stability and identity for young people. Juvenile delinquency climbed. So did the runaway population.

FLOWER CHILDREN

Many who left home during the 1960s did so for reasons other than family poverty. These runaways, mostly white and from affluent families, shunned the materialism their parents enjoyed. Former Harvard professor Timothy Leary, an advocate of illegal drugs, urged young people to "Tune in, turn on, drop out." What better way to drop out than to leave home?

The '60s runaways rejected not just their families, but society in general. Some ran away as a protest against the unpopular Vietnam War. Others rejected mainstream religions in favor of the spirituality they found from eastern religions. Many welcomed a new lifestyle that centered around open sex, illicit drugs, and psychedelic music.

Many runaways went to rural communes, living the farming life that their parents had rejected a generation before. Others moved to the cities, particularly on the East and West Coasts. San Francisco's Haight-Ashbury district became the most famous destination of these wanderers, who were known as hippies or flower children. A young runaway could find drugs, sex with willing partners, and a philosophy that stressed peace and love over conflict and money. The alternative lifestyle became so famous that tour buses stopped in Haight-Ashbury so that out-of-towners could gawk at the flower children.

Idealism ruled Haight-Ashbury during the 1967 "summer of love." The communal existence and philosophy, residents felt, would serve as a positive example to a country corrupted by materialism and engaged in an immoral war. Within two years, the district went sour. Overcrowding forced out many of the flower children. Bad drugs caused widespread illness. Others left because of a rapidly increasing crime rate. By the end of the 1960s, Haight-Ashbury's days as a capital for young runaway idealists was over. Many of those who flocked there eventually returned home. Since most doctors were considered part of the

"Establishment," young people avoided them. As a result, many brought back unwanted health souvenirs: drug-related hepatitis, lung infection, and venereal disease.

WHO ARE TODAY'S RUNAWAYS?

The U.S. government defines a runaway as someone under age 18 who leaves home at least overnight without a parent's or guardian's knowledge or permission. Statistically speaking, the typical runaway is a white girl 13 to 15 years old. She comes from a family of lower to moderate income, and she will be on the road only a short time.

In reality, however, there is no such thing as a typical runaway. More than one million young people flee from home every year. Runaways come in all shapes, sizes, and colors. They are largely from lower-income backgrounds, but people of all income levels are represented among those away from home who congregate on city streets. Nearly twice as many females as males run away from home, although males are more likely to be "throwaways" or "pushouts." Blacks and Hispanics are increasingly represented among those who flee.

Runaways are young, and the age for running appears to be decreasing. A U.S. government study claimed that the average age of runaways in federally funded shelters is just under 15 years, although children as young as 11 or 12 years have been admitted.

However, runaways are often the oldest child in their families. Their parents may use them to take care of younger brothers and sisters. They are forced to act as adults, even though they have not resolved their own adolescence. Such pressure may be too much for them.

Susan's mother often escaped her woes through bottles of tranquilizers. Her father, often absent, squandered family money on losing racehorses and other women. Susan ran away several times when young to escape unwanted responsibilities. At age 15, she left for good.

A black youth fleeing beatings from his alcoholic father might be a runaway. He might find himself on the streets next to a young Latina who is afraid to tell her parents of her pregnancy. The seemingly spoiled rich kid who has left the drab life of the suburbs might be sharing the sidewalk with a youngster whose parents have tossed him out of the house because they feel they can no longer afford to keep him. The loud-mouthed girl who slammed the door after sassing her parents during an argument last night might run into a boy who has been on the run for months. Or the boy might strike up a conversation with a girl who fled home to escape the continual sexual advances of her stepfather.

Statistically speaking, most of these runaways will return home within a day or two. Some will hang out longer before making peace with their parents

Reliable statistics on runaways do not exist. No one government agency deals with all runaway problems. Besides, many runaways are wary of all adults, particularly those they fear may send them back to a home they fled in the first place.

Some numbers are generally believed to be true. Most experts concede that more than one million persons under age 18 run away from their homes every year. Of those, between three fifths and two thirds are girls.

A 1989 study of homeless and runaway youth in federally funded shelters helps give a profile of runaways, as well as throwaway and other homeless young people. The study revealed the following information:

• 66 percent of runaway youth ages 10 to 17 came from two-parent homes, compared with 71 percent of youth throughout the country

• 85 percent of runaways lived with a parent or other adult during the previous year

• 85 percent of runaways lived with a parent just before coming to a shelter; 8 percent lived in a foster home or group home; 2 percent lived with friends; 2 percent lived in a correctional institution or jail; 2 percent lived on the street; and 1 percent lived independently

• 75 percent of runaways cited parents or other adults as their principal problem; 6 percent mentioned a family crisis; 4 percent said the juvenile justice system was their main problem, 4 percent cited other children or youth, 2 percent called school their chief problem, and 12 percent noted other personal problems

• 41 percent of the runaways that were surveyed claimed there was emotional conflict in the home; 29 percent complained about physical or sexual abuse; 29 percent said their parents were too strict; 18 percent cited parent neglect; 16 percent mentioned parental drug or alcohol abuse; and 8 percent mentioned domestic violence between parents; 40 percent of those polled cited multiple problems

• 63 percent of the runaways complained of depression; 50 percent mentioned school problems; 20 percent admitted to drug or alcohol abuse; 17 percent mentioned problems with the juvenile justice system; 12 percent said they were possibly suicidal; 6 percent cited pregnancy or veneral disease as a problem; 2 percent mentioned their sexuality as a cause for flight

The study covers those youths who stayed in federally funded homeless shelters. However, these figures do not necessarily represent runaways as a whole. For every runaway who goes to a shelter, an estimated five to ten avoid the shelters.

and coming back. Some never return home. Many head for what they see as the freedom and opportunities of big cities, but even smaller cities and small towns have these self-imposed exiles.

WHY DO THEY RUN?

There were about one million young runaways in 1980, compared with about 600,000 in 1970, although there were fewer teenagers in the United States in 1980 than 1970. The number of runaways has perhaps doubled since then. Why are they abandoning their homes?

Perhaps there are as many answers as there are runaways themselves. No doubt some of today's youth still run off to join the circus. And some reject the materialism of modern society. But romance and idealism are not the driving forces behind most of today's runaways.

For most, running becomes a way to cope with major personal or family problems. Many leave because of the by-products of poverty—alcohol or drug abuse, physical or mental abuse by frustrated parents. "In the 1960s, it was more common for kids to run to something—an environment or a lifestyle. Now they're running away from something," noted Cynthia Myers of the National Runaway Switchboard, a hotline that seeks to help runaways return home.

Teenagers run away for many different reasons. Sometimes they are escaping abusive family situations; sometimes school failure or a brush with the law is the cause.

Ray Jones of the Detroit Transit Alternative points out, "Early on we had a lot of the traditional runaway situations. There was the conflict in the home about going to college or staying up late or the young person was really just out to get a new experience. Now it is much more of a survival issue."

Sexual abuse is the most blatant cause of young people's flight. Young people, particularly girls, may fall victim to incest by a parent. Sometimes a trusted adult well known to the parents is the culprit. A stepfather may find his blossoming adolescent stepdaughter more sexually alluring than her plain middle-aged mother.

In many cases, sexual abuse has already taken place. A shelter director in Portland, Oregon, estimated that 85 percent of runaways in her shelter had been sexually abused at home.

"Pepper's" mother's boyfriend molested her when she was 6 years old. The mother later married a stepfather who raped her almost daily. She said the only way she could survive the assaults was to pretend "like I was on desert sand and what I was feeling was like water or rocks." She became pregnant by him at age 13. He paid for her abortion.

She tried telling her mother. The mother would not believe her because the assailant never left any bruises. Finally, she ran off to Boise, Idaho. She became a topless dancer and prostitute.

Her life on the outside turned out to be no more pleasant than the one she left. As a prostitute, she remained vulnerable to sexual attacks. "Rape is such a normal thing, it doesn't faze me," she said.

Stepfathers are not the only adults who take advantage of adolescent girls. Gabriela and Linda, two sisters, lived in a foster home. A friend of their foster mother's often visited them, accompanied by her husband. Over the years, the husband's attitude toward the girls evolved from friendly to flirtatious. One night he excused himself from his wife and her friend and cornered Gabriela in the basement. Not long after raping her, he went to Linda's room and began fondling her before she escaped. Then he returned to the living room as though nothing had happened. The two sisters compared notes, gathered up some belongings, and left the dangerous home.

Sometimes escape comes before an actual attack. Jane's stepfather became stricter and stricter with her. He accused her of having sex with lowlife scum, although she was not sexually active. One night he threatened to lock her in her room. Jane became convinced that he actually wanted her for himself. She ran before the stepfather had a chance to molest her.

Nonsexual violence poses another threat, particularly in households dominated by parental drug or alcohol abuse. For years, Cathy watched her mother and father fight after they drank too much. Occasionally, they hit her if she tried to make peace between them. One night, her father threw a bottle at her. When he threatened her at knifepoint, she ran.

Physical or sexual abuse can occur even in "good" families that are respected in the community. A father or mother active in church or civic affairs may be inflicting physical or psychological damage upon their children. The mask of respectability may hide family conflict. These parents may believe that since the community respects them, they must be raising their children properly.

"Self-confidence, ingenuity, and useful knowledge of how to seek help are necessary to cope with crises. Abusive parents seem to not have these abilities and any crisis has a greater impact upon them," says psychologist Brandt F. Steele. "If a crisis cannot be coped with adequately, it lasts longer, becomes more distressing, and can develop into an even more serious crisis. Eventually the situation may become disastrous and unmanageable. Parents become pushed beyond their strength, feel desperately hopeless, and end up abusing the child."

Few law enforcement or social work professionals openly congratulate children for running away from home. But they understand the motivations that would drive someone from an abusive situation. And they realize that some young people need to escape an unsafe environment. After listening to a girl's story of how she and her brothers and sisters received routine beatings from her parents, a New York social worker commented that her running was actually a healthy response. "That kid was the only sane member of her family—she ran away from it. She did the best thing she could do, leave," the social worker said.

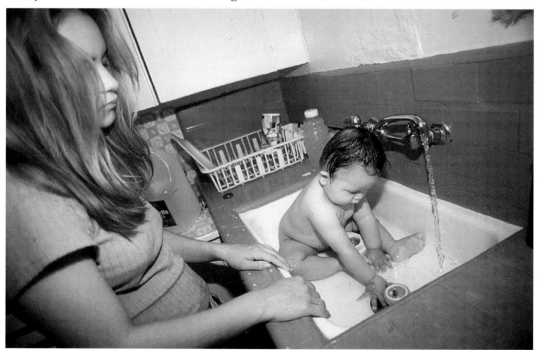

Added responsibilities at home, such as cooking for the family or caring for siblings, can overwhelm a teenager.

Reasons other than violence propel children from the home. An upcoming or recent divorce can shatter young persons' lives. At times they are led to believe that they caused the breakup. Sometimes the parents' separation leads to extra responsibilities. If the mother is forced to work, older children may become burdened with the added duties of caring for their younger brothers and sisters or doing extra chores. These burdens may become unbearable to someone already faced with school and social pressures.

"I was tired of being the middleman between my mom and my dad's divorce," says a Seattle runaway. "About a month after I got here I called my mom and said, 'How's it goin'?' She said, 'Oh, it's awful, you know. I'm broke. Your father is trying to drain me, make my life miserable.' I hung up on her and never called her again."

Custody battles may spur some young people to run away. A court may award custody of the child to one parent—the wrong parent, in the child's view. That child may go, without prior warning, to the parent of his or her choice. Or the youngster may unexpectedly shuttle back and forth between the divorced parents, playing one against the other, to get the best deal for him- or herself.

Occasionally the parent in a single-parent family remarries or otherwise finds a new partner. This new partner may be less than enthusiastic about sharing affection with the stepchild. The parent, forced to choose between the current romantic interest and a moody teenager, may reject the adolescent. These "couch homeless" may have a place to sleep, but no real family support in their lives. "Do they really have a home, or do they just have a couch when mom's boyfriend isn't there?" pondered Brian Love of Chicago's Night Ministry. Feeling unloved at home, they may seek companionship on the streets.

Sometimes the family structure simply disintegrates. This often occurs when one parent dies or abandons the family. A child may be thrown into a foster home, which may provide neither the love a child needs nor the memories that provide some stability.

Unreasonable restrictions drive many young people from foster homes and other institutions. Parents might have sent the youths to these homes because they could no longer handle them. Sometimes they were ordered there by a court. Even the threat of placement in one of these institutions may send a young person running.

Mike left a church-run home. He tried to return to his parents. But they were religious fundamentalists who feared he was becoming too worldly. Mike chafed at the thought of the restrictive school. When his parents threatened to return him there, he left their house as well.

James was placed in several foster homes and suffered in all of them. Then he decided he had had enough. "I was almost 13 at this point and I was getting pretty tired of living with people I didn't like and who didn't like me, so I decided to run away," he said.

Parental disapproval of sexual activity is one reason teens sometimes leave home. Another reason is disapproval of a particular girlfriend or boyfriend—the teens may run away to be together.

Sex, in many forms, forces young people from their homes. Conservative parents may have no tolerance for a sexually active son or (especially) a daughter. Some pregnant girls may fear the wrath of an angry parent and leave without telling their families. Others may tell their parents and get kicked out. A child of either gender who admits his or her homosexuality may find parents to be anguished, bewildered, and hostile.

Jennie was one such runaway. Pregnant at 14, she told her parents about the expected child. She said she felt good about having someone to hold. Her parents agreed that she should have the baby. But they would raise it as Jennie's brother or sister. Jennie was not to tell the child that she was the mother. Jennie could not stand the thought of such an arrangement. She ran.

Occasionally the sexual promiscuity that brings about the run is the parent's. "It has to be disconcerting if you wake up and don't know who will be in the kitchen drinking coffee with your mother," commented longtime Chicago caseworker Leonard de Montdrun.

School hassles form another major reason for young people to leave home. An adult may dismiss school problems as trivial unless he or she realizes that school is a young person's work. Five days a week for most of the year, young people see more of their teachers and classmates than their parents and families. School is a major source of praise or humiliation, of belonging or rejection. It is not only the failing students who are frustrated. Some otherwise good students who do not achieve perfection may be depressed by their school life. It is not surprising that many students run away in May or June—just before the school year's final report cards come out.

Sometimes learning disabilities indirectly trigger runaways. "They can't learn, and it's embarassing to them," said Paul Sullivan of YouthCare, a Seattle agency dealing with runaways. "Instead of admitting they can't learn, they act out in order to camouflage the deficiency. They dress weird or act weird. When the school or the parents don't resolve their problems, they run. It isn't that the parents aren't supportive. They just may not have the ability to recognize what's going on."

Unfeeling teachers and school officials may contribute to a student's sense of worthlessness that may bring about a run. "School—there was a nightmare," said Terri, a Maryland runaway. "Everybody was picking on me 'cause I was in a foster home and stuff . . . I'd just sit in school and ask myself, 'Why does everybody hate me so much?' It was the teachers, too. They wouldn't help me . . . They were like, 'This girl ain't no good, she's in a foster home, she's a troublemaker.'"

"The kids usually have one bad problem after another in school," explained a New York youth worker. "Marks, discipline, attendance, and so on. Many of their friends also have problems and they support each other. Pretty soon it makes little sense for them to go to class, so they don't. Day after day is spent around school, but none actually attends . . . Eventually the school begins to ignore the kid and after a point the kid feels he doesn't have to attend. No one tells them not to attend. They simply stop showing up."

Even teenagers with no thought of leaving home rebel against overly strict parents. Adolescents know they are growing; they no longer wish to be treated like children. When they make what seems to them a reasonable request or statement, a rejection followed by "because I say so" or "that's the way I was raised" is not a sufficient response. Some teens may bristle at impossible curfews or household work that leaves them no time for their friends. Some may protest if a parent tries to keep them from dating someone of another race or religion.

Other demands may seem minor by comparison. Keep your room clean. Stop smoking. Do better in school. Do your chores. Arguments can arise between parents and young people over anything from pierced ears to skipping church to going to a basketball game on a school night to daughter's (or mother's) new boyfriend.

Harsh parents may start a cycle that chases a youngster from the home. If a young person gets into trouble, these parents often respond with punishments and beatings. This leads to resentment and more trouble, which leads to more punishment. Parents become increasingly disappointed in the child. They act as though the child will never amount to anything, and the child lives down to their expectations. The child, feeling hopelessly inadequate, abandons hope of living with the parents. At that time, he or she runs away.

Of course, one person's definition of strict may be another's definition of reasonable. Fifteen-year-old Katie bolted from her home because her parents would not let her stay out until 3:00 a.m. on weekends—a curfew hour most teenagers would have a hard time justifying.

Overly permissive parents may cause as much resentment as harsh ones. Some parents may think they are fooling their children by giving them unbridled freedom. But seeming tolerance in their kids' lifestyle choices may hide a lack of interest in the youngsters' well-being. Many young people see this attitude as the parents' way of saying, "Do anything you want, but just leave me alone." People from such environments may survive on the streets but often have trouble establishing meaningful relationships with their fellow street people.

After Ellie's mother died, her father threw himself into his business. He gave Ellie money and material goods, but little attention or affection. She attended the best boarding schools and was served by maids, but saw her father only on vacations. When she turned 14, she decided to surprise him by paying him a visit at his Chicago office.

Instead of being delighted by the visit, the father was infuriated. He reserved a ticket for her on the next available flight back to New York. There a servant would meet her and return her to school. Ellie boarded the plane but escaped detection at the New York airport. She was never seen again.

A parent who lets a child do what he or she wants may be frustrated, not permissive. That parent may run out of patience or energy. Discipline doesn't work. Discussion doesn't work. Maybe counseling doesn't work. The parent gives up trying and sinks into passivity. The child, tired and frustrated at being ignored, exits the unhappy home.

Some runaways leave one step ahead of the law. They already may be using or even dealing drugs. They may be involved in theft. A youth whose parents threaten to call the authorities will depart before the parents make good on their threat.

Friends may come between a runaway and his or her parents. Parents may all but force their kids to choose between their friends or them. If the parents and the young people have problems already, there is no choice. An adolescent will go with someone who at least understands peer group concerns over someone who does not understand anything at all.

These same friends may also serve as examples to a would-be runaway. If they could leave home and survive, why can't I? Jesse, a California runaway, said, "I never really did think much about moving out until I see this guy Ralph do it. Nothing happened to him, he just left. I thought the cops would get him but nobody bothered him . . . If everybody's doing it, I say why not me?"

Some of those who leave lower-income families may do so to help their

Experimentation with drugs and alcohol is a major source of conflict between parents and teenagers. Young people may feel mature enough to handle drinking long before their parents, or the law, permit it.

cash-starved parents. In some cases, young people are not angry with their parents when they run away. They are trying to escape impoverished inner city or rural environments. The youths may feel they are helping their parents by easing a financial burden. Parents often understand or even support the child's decision.

The homes runaways leave seldom have only one problem. Drug or alcohol abuse often contribute to many of the others. The alcoholic father may also be physically or sexually abusive. A study of youths in San Francisco clinics showed that 75 percent of runaways came from homes with multiple problems. That compared with only 10 or 15 percent of the general population.

At the heart of all problems between parents and their children is a lack of communication. Portland, Oregon, policeman Brad Bailey comments, "A home structure consists of one or more parents providing the child with the essential elements that make a child into an adult." The ability to communicate joys and concerns is one of those important elements. Most teenagers will try to please their parents. But they are not psychics. They cannot always understand what goes on in Mom or Dad's mind. They will try to please their parents without success only so many times. Then they give up.

Parents often complain that they can't "get through" to their adolescent children. Teenagers and pre-teens often say the same thing about their parents. If family members cannot talk things out, the younger members may try other tactics to make their problems known. They may plead with parents, act out, go through rapid character changes. And if these mechanisms don't work, they may run away. If they return home and the problems are still not resolved, the youths may flee home again.

THROWAWAYS AND PUSHOUTS

Even teens who plan their run for months take little with them and seldom have much money. They often leave town the cheap and anonymous way—by hitchhiking.

Krista's father deserted her and her mother. Krista and her mother then lived out of a motel room, where the mother made a living by prostitution. One day they got into an argument.

"She told me to leave," Krista said. "She was wasted. So I left. It had happened a few times before; she would kick me out and then I'd come back when she was sober and everything would be fine. But it was different this time. She was saying, 'You're old enough to take care of yourself. Go out and get a job. Get away from me. You make me sick.'"

Krista left the motel and came back an hour later. If she expected apologies from her mother, she was mistaken. "She opened the door and said, 'Leave! Leave! I told you to leave!'" Krista said.

She went away again, this time for three hours. "Then I went back again. This time no one answered when I knocked on the door. I opened the door and walked in. Everything was gone. All my clothes, everything. The place was empty. I guess she just drove off."

Joey faced a similar situation. He lived in a trailer with two indifferent parents. An observer described the trio as "a group of people who lived together because they had nowhere else to go."

One day, the parents went. Joey came home and found the door locked. When he opened it, only his clothes were inside. Joey moved in with some neighbors and never tried to locate his parents.

Krista and Joey were no runaways. Their parents ran from them. Both fell into a category known as throwaways or pushouts. These are minors who do not leave without their parents' permission. The U.S. Department of Health and Human Services defines throwaways as minors who leave home at the encouragement or discretion of a parent or guardian. Pushouts are just that—persons under 18 who are forced out of their homes.

There are four main types of throwaways. Some (the pushouts) were ordered to leave the home. Others left home, and the caretaker refused to take them back. A third group are runaways whose parent or guardian made no attempt to recover them. The last group were abandoned or deserted.

What offenses did these exiles commit? They might have gotten pregnant, started drinking or using drugs, talked back once too often, eaten too much. In some cases, they became a financial burden. Perhaps they could not get along with the parent's new boyfriend or girlfriend. Maybe the parents just plain got tired of them. Or maybe the parents never wanted them at all. In all cases, the parents found it easier to remove the child from the house than to resolve family problems.

Numbers of throwaways and pushouts are even harder to determine than runaways. Some of these hapless youth are literally shoved out the door. Parents are reluctant to report them to the police. If those parents had wanted the kids in the home, they would not have pressured them out in the first place. Also, the difference between throwaways and runaways is often negligible. A father who continually beats his son may not be directly ordering him out, but the beatings send more than a slight signal that the boy is not welcome in the home.

Judith Buey, director of the National Network of Runaway and Youth Services, commented in 1984, "Ten years ago, if parents could not cope, they'd just place the children somewhere until they could cope. Now they just decide they didn't want the kids around anymore."

A caseworker at The Door, a Manhattan agency, said, "Some parents are no longer considering a 16-year-old a kid. [These kids] are being forced to grow up and take care of themselves."

As many as one third to one half of all runaways may be throwaways or pushouts. These young people provide a special problem for police, shelters, and social service agencies. Even if the parents could be persuaded to take them back, the youths face a devastating environment and even physical abuse. More likely, the throwaways and their parents or guardians will never reunite. In New York City, some shelters have shifted their emphasis from runaways to throwaways and pushouts. Runaways at least have a home where they can return. Throwaways and pushouts have nothing.

WHERE DO THEY RUN?

In earlier times, runaways might have gone hundreds of miles. They set off to sea or joined the buffalo hunters. Nowadays, most venture only a few miles from home. Most still feel attachment to their families. Most want to—and do— go back. If their aim is to return home, there is no reason to go too far from it.

There are other reasons most runaways do not go far. It takes time, money, and energy to travel. Airplanes and trains are out of the budget for most runaways. Buses cost money for long, tiring rides. Only a tiny percentage of runaways have their own cars.

Hitchhiking is free, although food breaks along the way quickly eat up a hitcher's dollars. Twenty years ago, hitchhikers were common sights along many American roads. But mutual suspicion grew between hitchers and motorists. How do I know this man (or woman) picking me up won't rob or assault me? How do I know this hitchhiker won't pull a knife or gun and steal my car? These concerns greatly cut down the number of hitchhikers. Besides, the person picking up the hitchhiker may be a police officer who will send the hitchhiking runaway back home.

Several young people's meccas attract runaways. Thousands flock each year to New York City, despite the city's often-frightening reputation. Police estimate that between 10,000 and 20,000 runaways inhabit the Times Square area. Middle-class runaways join college students and other spring break vacationers in Fort Lauderdale, Florida. California, with its warm weather and beaches, lures many young drifters. Hollywood dreams attract runaways to Los Angeles, and some with the hippie spirit still go to San Francisco. Chicago attracts midwestern runaways. Seattle in recent years has drawn young runaways. But many others go to smaller cities. These places attract young people who want more adventure than they found back home, yet shudder at the thought of living in a big city.

For most, particularly in affluent communities, the run is a short-term affair. The runner generally feels good about his family but walks out over a particular gripe. The youth who receives a loud lecture from his or her parents about coming home late might show the parents who's boss by storming out the door and not coming back at all. This dramatic gesture might make the appropriate point, particularly if the youth has an available friend or relative with an extra bed or couch handy.

Usually an adult at the friend or relative's house will phone the home and let the parents know that the runaway is all right. The young arguer may demonstrate his or her independence, get a comfortable night's sleep, and maybe even return home in time for breakfast. Such a casual runaway situation could happen in almost any family.

All may end up well. Then again, the underlying problems that lead to a verbal sparring match may not be resolved. The arguments may continue,

Places where lots of young people congregate are good places for runaways. Cities with mild weather are especially popular. New Orleans, Seattle, Fort Lauderdale, and Los Angeles all have large runaway populations.

becoming louder and more frequent. A runaway pattern may emerge, with flights becoming longer and commoner. Returns home may become less and less cordial. Finally, the youth affected may run off—and not come back.

SPOTTING A POTENTIAL RUNAWAY

Teenagers seldom tell their parents "I'm going to run away tomorrow" and then make good on the threat the next day. But often, young people give signs that they may run.

A certain amount of rebellion is normal for any adolescent. He or she wants to discover the outside world and test the limits of what the parents are willing to tolerate. Most parents realize that changes are part of adolescence. It is not the end of the world.

But if issues at home seem severe enough to a young person, he or she will try to communicate their concerns. If the concerns are not addressed, they may take flight from home.

Here are a few signs of a possible runaway:

Sudden behavior changes. Parents may observe "overnight" behavior changes that actually may have been occurring over months. A onetime high school honors student now shows little interest in grades. A kid who once dressed conservatively may now sport green hair or rings all over his or her body. A previously responsible kid now "forgets" to do things. These are all signs of children who may be facing major problems at home. Perhaps they have tried to relate their problems to their parents. When verbal attempts failed, they resorted to nonverbal means of communication.

Inability to tolerate frustration. Patience sometimes disappears. Everything has to come to the teen, and it has to come right now! The inability to delay gratification produces a young person unable to get along with others, who can neither understand nor be understood by adults or peers. This impulsive person will act without warning.

Changes in relationships. He or she used to have lifelong friends. Now they no longer seem important. Instead, the teenager has a newer and less desirable circle of friends, and may hang around with this group to the exclusion of everyone else. On the other hand, they may stay home and ignore peers completely.

A sudden change in behavior or appearance can indicate that someone is deeply troubled and may be planning to run away.

Suddenly, all adults may be the subject of suspicion. This applies not only to parents, but also to previously trusted persons such as older relatives, teachers, counselors, or clergy. Parents may see a sudden unwillingness in their children to confide in them. Adults, to these young people, simply cannot and do not understand their problems. Any parental rules and restrictions seem excessive.

Signs of depression. Does an adolescent feel and act as though he or she is worthless? Are there signs of drug or alcohol abuse? Have grades plummeted in recent terms? Is there a feeling of hopelessness? Does he or she frequently fantasize about how everything will suddenly get better? Does he or she believe that some particular action will instantly solve all of their problems?

Poor performance in school. For most young people, performance in school is a major part of their identity. Unexpectedly bad grades may be a cause for flight. Inability to get along with teachers or classmates may sink students into depression. The results may be a loss of interest in studying, behavior problems, absenteeism, and eventually a run from home.

Verbal statements about running away. At one time or another, almost every child has threatened to run away. Some young kids have actually "run away" by going around the block and returning before their parents knew they were gone. Usually, such words are idle talk. But if a young person feels no support from parents, or faces physical threats, these words may be serious. A threat to run may be a cry for help. Surveys have shown that more than half of all runaways discuss their plans with someone before leaving. Just because someone says they will run away or has made the threat before, is no reason to ignore them.

No matter how they left—runaway, throwaway, or pushout—young people who leave home find themselves in similar, uncertain situations. Serious runaways—those who leave more than overnight and for reasons more intense than a minor family spat—seldom do so on the spur of the moment. A drastic move like leaving home is often something that has been contemplated for weeks and months. The flight from home comes as a response to a long-running problem that has no end in sight.

Even though they have considered fleeing for a long time, most runaways depart with few possessions and even fewer plans. After a few days away from home, their money and often their possessions dwindle. Broke, bedraggled, and without much apparent hope, many runaways live marginal lives on city streets and town squares.

Why do they stay in such an existence? If their life on the streets is worse than the one they left behind, they would return home. As a Chicago street kid named Sunshine put it, "Most people aren't out here because they wake up one morning and think, 'Hey, I think it would be fun to be homeless.

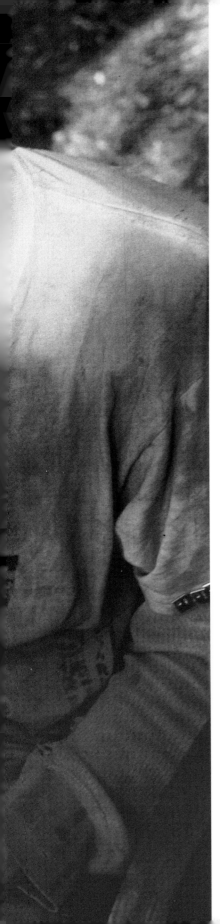

2

LIFE ON THE STREETS

*They know the code of the street, the scams, the places to get a
hot meal, clean clothes, illegal drugs.*
—Vivian Lou Chen, *Portland Oregonian*

The runaway has made the move. He or she has packed up belongings, taken that first step out of the house, then the second and the third. A question enters the runaway's mind: Now what?

The first problem is a very immediate one—where to spend the night. No concern, except perhaps for food, is greater than the need for a place to crash, or stay informally for little or no money.

Many runaways first flee to their friends. After all, their friends are the ones who know their problems, their concerns, their needs. Their friends are the ones who can provide the moral support that their families cannot or do not give.

Staying with friends, however, can have drawbacks. Most important among the obstacles are the friends' parents. Some runaways skirt this problem by avoiding the parents altogether. They either go to the friends when the parents are out of town, or wait until the parents are asleep, sneak into the house, and leave before the parents wake up the next day. In some cases, runaways may sleep outside at night, but go to a friend's house for a shower and a meal while the friends' parents are at work.

When the friends' parents are aware of the runaway's presence, tensions may arise. Often, the parents do not want to become involved with the runaway's problems. Some conservative parents

*Runaways on the street don't always know where their next
meal is coming from. They eat whatever they can scavenge.*

may view a runaway as a threat, someone whose values are different than those they are trying to instill in their own children.

Sometimes, the friends' parents may not be actively hostile. But astute runaways can pick up clues. Seventeen-year-old Jennie noted, "No one really said anything, and that was the problem . . . I mean people were a pain, without even trying to be. They just sort of told you they didn't want you there without having to say so."

Even if the parents remain cordial, the friends may burn out on hosting a runaway twenty-four hours a day. Friends, after all, have their own problems, needs, and lives. A runaway may find that even the closest of companions may tire of helping, being inconvenienced, or straining a relationship with their own parents. And a runaway who decides to move out from a friend's house may not be welcome if he or she decides to return.

Runaways' own attitudes may turn them off friends. Robert, an 18-year-old, observed, "You get in a bad mood and you start acting funny around people. Nobody wants you around them after a while. You begin to put people in a bad head. You don't get any good messages from people . . . I mean, who wants somebody around who is a drag? You usually find out people got their own problems, so they don't need yours."

Occasionally, a teenager may shuttle back and forth between family and friends, or move from friend to friend. One commented, "When I need cash, I always go to my brother or his wife. I try to pay them back, but I know they will give it to me anyway. . . . He comes up with a little cash, and I don't have to stay over. Now I got some money and a place to stay, since I know I can stay with my friends anyway."

If friends are not available, then runaways may go to other family members. But staying with kin offers advantages and disadvantages. On the plus side, family members know the runaway well. They usually know the reasons that set the person to running, and they know the person well enough that he or she can act naturally around them. They offer a secure place to stay, and the runner is not likely to be kicked out of the house. Runaways need not worry about fending off outsiders, and they can cool off there before deciding to return home or go somewhere else.

On the other hand, the runaways' relatives are also relatives of the parents. Most likely, they have heard the parents' side of the runaway's story. They may not be sympathetic to the runaway's plight or may not want to get involved with it. Or they may try to pressure the runaway into returning home, when he or she may not be ready to do so.

Sometimes runaways stay with unlikely relatives—their own parents. A juvenile court ruled that Leticia's parents were unfit to raise her. Leticia disagreed. She fled her court-appointed foster home and returned to her biological parents.

IF A FRIEND RUNS

You are at home on a quiet weekday evening, studying or just hanging around. Your parents are out. The doorbell rings. Your best friend needs a place to stay. He or she will not go home. Your friend wants to talk and asks if you have some time. What do you do?

• Do something. The worst thing you can do is say "Go home!" or "Go away!" Pretending that there is no problem only makes the situation worse. Besides, the person came to you as a friend. Your friend would not have contacted you if he or she did not value your opinion.

• If your friend needs a place to stay, find one. Does he or she have any understanding relatives nearby? If the friend wants to stay on your couch, preset limits to how long he or she may stay. Benjamin Franklin once wrote, "Dead fish and visitors smell in three days."

• Listen carefully to the entire story before forming an opinion. Stop and ask questions if something in the story is not clear. Try to see if you can get the story from the parent's point of view. Why did they do (or not do) what they did?

• Consider the problem and whether it could be avoided. If the parent is angry about a runaway's drug use, there is an obvious solution to this problem: Stop using drugs.

• If your friend talks about running, discuss realities of life on the road. Talk about how much money will be needed. Ask where your friend will stay, how he or she plans to survive. Point out possible health and safety hazards. Mention some of the negative consequences of running.

• Seek outside help. If the runaway might consider returning home, find a neutral third party, such as a teacher or minister, to act as an intermediary between the runaway and his or her parents.

If a return home is out of the question, seek other help. Local hotlines, shelters, or social agencies will be listed under Social Service Organizations in the telephone directory's yellow pages. These organizations can provide not only a place to stay, but they may provide counseling that your friend needs.

While with those parents, she led the life of a fugitive. She could not leave her parents' home for fear of being discovered by the authorities. "I hid out," she said. "There was always somebody knocking at the door looking for me—detectives, cops, social workers, the whole bit."

For many runaways, staying with family members is not an option. A large percentage of runaways are the oldest children in their families. They lack the oasis that an older brother or sister's home can provide. For them, and many others, if staying with friends is not possible, then the only choice is the streets.

Runaways traveling together are more likely to head out on their own than to seek family or friends. Girls, more than boys, are likely to leave with a partner. The companion may be a lover or a girlfriend. Boys, whether fleeing an intolerable home situation, escaping delinquency problems, or simply seeking adventure, usually flee alone.

Usually, it takes a while for a newly fleeing youth to find a reliable sleeping spot. Fourteen-year-old Jonah recalled, "In the past ten days I have made six changes. I wish I could get a regular place to stay. The first two days I stayed with [a friend], but that canceled out. From last week, it's been the train, the YMCA, and the shelter."

Some runaways become urban nomads, staying no more than a night or two at a time in any given place. One night it could be a park bench, the next night underneath a railroad trestle or in an alley, the following night the basement of an abandoned building. A youth on the run may spend the night roaming the streets or sipping a cup of coffee at an all-night diner. One with a few bucks might nap for a few hours in a late-night movie theater. A small percentage of lucky runaways may have a car that can double as a personal motel.

Billy, in New York, lived in cars for a year. He would break into one, jump-start it to get the heater and radio running, and sleep there. If the car's owner or police discovered him, he would move to another car.

Eventually, many find a "squat"—an abandoned building that serves as an apartment. These unsafe, condemned buildings usually lack even the barest

With no place to go and no money for shelter, runaways sleep wherever they can: in parks, alleys, abandoned buildings, on subway trains or in bus stations.

necessities. There is no gas or electricity or water. A runaway may find dozens of unofficial roommates in adjoining apartments. In addition to the human roommates, rats and cockroaches often overrun the squats.

Once a runaway finds a place to stay—even the dreariest of squats—he or she claims it as strongly as does any homeowner. Most runaways try to avoid violence. But sometimes violence does not avoid them. "You have to learn how to fight, one way or another, or you disappear," commented a Seattle runaway.

The squats may be uninhabitable to most people, but many runaways appreciate anyplace where they can live undisturbed. Most Los Angeles residents suffered from a 1994 earthquake that forced numerous buildings to be abandoned. A runaway named Troll welcomed the disaster. "It freed up a lot of housing for us," he explained.

Many runaways—both male and female—willingly trade sex for a place to stay with sugar daddies (or rarely, sugar mamas). These relationships are seldom permanent, and the runaway is soon looking for shelter again.

A very lucky runaway might find a hassle-free room with a stranger. A Chicagoan named Heidi offered free apartments to runaways. In turn, she asked sweat equity: her guests were expected to keep the place clean and do chores.

Heidi, however, had little use for those not in legitimate need. "I took in a girl from the suburbs once," she said. "The girl came in the next day carrying fifty dollars worth of groceries. Then she was flirting and sleeping with the boys here. I take in a lot of kids whose parents were alcoholics or who beat them. But she had a nice and fair family and just couldn't tolerate them. I kicked her out."

Most runaways, if they find hosts, meet people with considerably less to offer than Heidi. Like many eastern runaways, Tim headed to Grand Central Station in New York City. He found a kindly friend who gave all he had—which was not much. The shriveled derelict led him to a hidden opening in the station. From there, they descended a 20-foot ladder to a dark passageway. They walked several hundred feet to a space the older man claimed. There the man heated a can of stew on a warm pipe and gave it to Tim.

The next day, they climbed up to the station and washed themselves in its bathroom. The good-hearted man invited Tim back to his "home" that evening. But within an hour, Tim was on his way back home.

HANGING OUT

Once a runaway gets settled somewhere, he or she may wonder what to do next. The answer may be nothing, but a very important nothing. Next to sleeping, many runaways spend most of their time simply hanging out.

What is hanging out? Almost any unorganized activity not related to direct survival. Runaways hang out in squats, parks, runaway shelters, public transportation, or anywhere else they can avoid hassles.

The amount of money they have and the security of their living conditions may determine where they hang out. People without a place to stay may be too busy getting themselves settled to hang out much. Those with a little income may choose hangouts where they spend a bit of money.

Ann Russell runs a coffee-house in suburban Chicago that attracts many local teenagers. Some of these are runaways, Russell admits, although she does not ask them if they are.

"They hang out in the coffee-house's downstairs section, talking or playing board games," she noted. "They usually come in after school hours, and typically hang out until closing time. They may nurse a cup of coffee all night. Generally, they're a little loud, but they don't seem obnoxious. They're kids. Police officers will come by every couple of weeks or so carrying a runaways' picture. They'll ask me, 'Do you know this kid?' Some of them have been here."

Runaway teens often spend their first few days away with friends, but they usually have to move on soon. They can end up living illegally in squats—abandoned, often dangerous buildings without heat, water, and electricity.

Hangouts also may vary with the amount of time someone is away from home. At first, some runaways stay near places where they spent time while living at home. They may still linger around the schoolyard, recreation center, or shopping mall. But as time goes on and they place distance between themselves and their previous lives, these hangouts are replaced by other locations more important to their new lifestyle.

Hanging out may look like a low-energy pastime. But it serves a valuable function for someone away from home. This informal time with other runaways and street people serves as their newspaper, television, and radio. From the people who casually wander in and out of a hanging-out group, a runaway can learn important information for survival. Where do the police hassle young people? Are there any jobs available? What runaway centers are nearby? How can I get a free meal?

"I spent one cold night in Boston," recalled Barbara, a New England runaway. "It was my first night. I was particularly broke, but the next day I met people—kids who knew their way around. They were really nice. Told me the best places to panhandle, where the good corners are, the ones to hang out at when there's a lunch break in the big buildings. They told me about the place I'm crashing in now."

Veteran runaways may tell horror stories of the street or road to their younger counterparts. They may relate tales of abuse at the hands of anything from the court system to a local street gang. Then again, they may tell boastful stories which may or may not be true. Newer runaways learn two valuable lessons from these old-timers. First, it is possible to live away from home. Second, it can be dangerous.

Hanging out serves as more than an information source. At the very least, it kills time. At its best, it can be a lot of fun. After a stressful life at home, what could be better than visiting with friendly people, exchanging stories and relaxing?

Hanging out also helps runaways learn necessary new skills. Successful street people must be able to exchange old friends for new ones and develop new personalities for each different situation. They must be able to spot trouble or potential trouble. They must be able to shift gears and make a quick change in plans if something better comes along. These skills can be learned from the street's informal "teachers."

Runaways often find their hanging-out partners are more tolerant than the people back home. "I told everybody I was gay. Nobody ragged me for it," commented Bettina, who ran from Baltimore to Los Angeles. "That was nice. And I didn't have to worry about guys trying to move in on me. It's a strange thing about the streets, believe it or not. There's a lot of people you can trust—I know it's an odd thing to say, but it's true . . . . Some of the street people are just more trustworthy than some 'normal' people."

Runaways at an intermediate, or exploratory stage, are those most likely to hang out. A youth new in town or fleeing a bad situation finds survival to be an immediate concern. He or she needs to spend time and energy getting settled somewhere. At the other extreme, well-established runaways have jobs or other activities. They lack the time to do nothing for hours on end.

After a while, hanging out becomes stale. Even the least motivated of runaways can stand only so much of doing nothing. A runaway named Robert commented, "After a while, you can just sit around with your friends so long. I mean hanging out is okay and all, but . . . you can't get over by sitting there. I need a job more than I need to sit around."

Just surviving on the street can be exhausting and depressing. When they're not search-ing for food, a place to stay, or other necessities, most runaways just hang out.

STREET FAMILIES

As the runaways' lives change, so do their social situations. All but the most diehard loners eventually find a street family, an unofficial group of similar souls with common backgrounds and needs.

Street families provide a closeness that many never found with their fam-ilies at home. The emotional, financial, and even sexual support that most crave is now available. New street family members get the feeling that someone cares about them and will take care of them. "One of the things that inspired me is how much they hug each other," Rev. Lee Lowrey commented about one Chicago street family. "The hugging is genuine."

"Anyone who wants to be here is welcome," said Joy, a member of a street family of "35 to 40 people." She noted, "If someone who wants to hang around wants to come to us, we are pleased to have them."

A runaway may hang around with several groups before finding a street family that makes them feel comfortable. They may shop around for street fami-lies the way adults shop for cars. Runaways often had fragile identities at home.

With different street families, they can adopt different personalities or even names, until they find one that suits them.

But once he or she finds a street family, loyalty to it can be fierce. "I've got a place to be, a family who cares about me," said Sunshine, a Chicago runaway. "This is my family. I love the people here."

Street families can provide physical as well as mental security. Newly arrived runaways are nervous about their belongings, with good reason. A trusted street family member may give that runaway a place to stow his or her stuff while looking for a job or food.

People within the street family often assume the roles of those within traditional families. A casual observer can see who is the strong father figure, the helpful big sister, and so on. Previous "younger brothers" who once depended on veteran runaways for help become "older brothers" who give the same help to those who just arrived on the streets. A friendly young woman named Nikki calls herself a "mother hen" to many Chicago runaways. "Literally thousands of children come to me," she said.

Street family members look after their own. "One [roommate] looked like she had [hepatitis] and she didn't know it," said Steve, a Los Angeles runaway. "I told her she'd better have it checked out—but she was afraid to. I looked up all the necessary information about hepatitis through my own connections, and then convinced her to go to the doctor."

These street families have no blood relationships, nor do they have any formal agreements. But there are certain unwritten rules that everyone knows. If you have a surplus of anything, even an extra donut, you give it to someone who doesn't have anything. Protect each other from outsiders, including legal authorities. Stealing from the grocery store may be tolerated by some, but no one ever steals anything from another family member. Some members or would-be members are gradually shunned because they are too obnoxious. Since there is no official membership, there are no official penalties for breaking the rules. But anyone who violates the rules soon finds himself or herself alone again—exiled from the street family.

Not all street families provided good results for runaways. One of the most famous families of runaways inhabited the southern California desert in the late 1960s. A drifter and small-time criminal named Charles Manson attracted dozens of young girls and boys to his remote ranch. Manson's family lived by begging and theft. The cultlike group followed a bizarre belief that a race war would develop, and Manson and his followers would end up ruling the country. Manson claimed that songs from Beatles albums sent him cryptic messages.

In order to start the race war, Manson sent his followers to murder several prominent Los Angeles residents. Actress Sharon Tate and six others died in two nights of grisly killings. Eventually, Manson was caught and sentenced to life in prison.

Even the strongest of street families have limited life spans. Sometimes the leader who holds the family together goes elsewhere. Maybe a fight between family members poisons the whole group. Anything from an unexpected pregnancy to an arrest may shake up the group. Surviving members may re-form the street family or scatter in many different directions.

Many runaways who do not belong to street families may hook up with a partner for awhile. This partnership may last only for a hitchhiking trip, or the partners may live together for a longer time. Often one partner will be a few years older. The older partner provides wisdom and experience while enjoying the company of his or her younger mate.

A Seattle runaway explained his reason for joining up with someone else. "Everyone, no matter how big or tough they are, should always have a partner," he said. "You never want to go on the streets alone. It's a mistake. It's just that you get lonely, you get upset, you get beat up. . . . You can never tell if someone's gonna come up in front of you and get your attention and some dude's gonna come up behind you and bust your head. Partners are better."

SEX, DRUGS, AND ALCOHOL

Life is not milk and cookies for young people on the streets. Many runaways get involved with alcohol or illegal drugs. Most are sexually active. Often, this is the behavior which caused problems at home in the first place. And often, the stressful events at home made them vulnerable to alcohol, drug, and sex problems.

Whether they want to get slightly high or end up in a stupor, most runaways can find alcohol. Older friends may pass liquor on to them. In many cases, irresponsible store or tavern owners knowingly sell beer or wine to underage customers.

A 1991 survey showed that 42 percent of homeless youth (including runaways and throwaways) currently drank alcohol. Almost half of them had had a drink within the past thirty days. A third of the drinkers showed symptoms of alcoholism, including getting into fights and not remembering events of the previous night.

Many runaways find drugs as easily available as alcohol. They may indulge in marijuana, cocaine, heroin, or any of a number of other street drugs. They may indulge to get high, or to waste themselves away. Sometimes they start with the first intention, and over time it leads to the second.

For some of the runaways, drug or alcohol abuse is nothing new. If they did not experience it themselves, their parents did. Ginger Boggett, director of a Portland, Oregon, center for runaways, noted "Parents' drug use within families is a much more serious problem than before. A lot of kids get involved as a direct result of what they see at home."

Since drug use is frequently one reason for running away, it's not surprising that marijuana, cocaine, and other drugs are common among street kids. Alcohol is also very common—one study showed that nearly half of all runaways drink alcohol.

Why do runaways become involved with drugs or alcohol? In some cases, they enjoy the high feeling a beer or a marijuana cigarette may bring. Often peer pressure plays a role. Junelle, a Portland runaway, said she would like to stop taking drugs, but "people I hang around with do it all night."

Other reasons are deadlier to the mind and body. Junelle said she buys drugs off the street to ease hunger pangs. "Food comes last," she explained.

Some runaways intoxicate themselves to escape the hell their lives have become. Father Bruce Ritter, former director of New York City's Covenant House, recalled a 17-year-old male prostitute who turned to alcohol. "He drinks because that is what he has to do to survive," Father Ritter said of the young hustler.

Sex plays even more of a role in most runaways' lives than drugs or alcohol. Many girls flee home rather than tell their parents of their pregnancies. Others, especially boys, run because their parents cannot accept their homosexuality. Most runaways were sexually active before they left home. Once on the run, almost all engage in some form of sexual activity, leading to high rates of pregnancy among runaway teens.

A pregnant runaway may not be happy at home, but she poses problems for herself and the child when she leaves. Most likely, she does not get the nutrition or rest needed for a healthy child. She may not get proper medical attention. The result could be an impoverished, undernourished, unhealthy baby.

Much of the sexual intimacy is high-risk activity. Runaways, much more than other teenagers, have unprotected sex. They may sleep with multiple partners, prostitutes, or intravenous drug users. They may be victims of sexual assault. This high-risk sex may lead to sexually transmitted diseases. A Minnesota study of runaways showed that 40 percent had a communicable sexual disease. One out of eight were unaware that their sexual partners carried a disease.

HEALTH

Few if any young people need basic health services more than those on the run from home. They are often victims of physical and sexual abuse and family chaos. Yet the ones who need health care most often have the least access to it. If they do have that access, they often fail to use it.

Juveniles on the street fall prey to a number of health problems: malnutrition, respiratory infections, sexually transmitted diseases, pregnancy, substance abuse, and mental illness. They suffer everything from hepatitis to tooth decay and gum disease. A recent Los Angeles survey showed that runaways were more likely than nonrunaways to suffer from uncontrolled asthma, pneumonia, pelvic inflammatory disease, drug abuse, and trauma.

The most obvious problem deals with nutrition. Runaways seldom have much money. Like most other impoverished people, they do not eat well. A runaway who begs, borrows, steals, or Dumpster-dives for food seldom gets three square meals a day. The food they do get is often fast food or junk food, not nutritionally balanced meals.

AIDS is a real-life nightmare for young people on the run. Intravenous drug abuse is rampant in some areas where runaways gather. If they share needles, they run the risk of contracting AIDS and other communicable diseases. Even those who do not take drugs put themselves at risk by having sex with those who do. The consequences are deadly. AIDS claims the lives of many persons in their twenties, which means they first contracted the illness during their teenage years. Of twelve youths recently found in a Hollywood squat and brought in for testing, half were HIV-positive.

Mental illness in its many forms affects runaways. This is not surprising, given their situation. They started their run with problems severe enough to drive them from home. Add their present problems (such as lack of nutrition, substance abuse, poor hygiene, no money, and little hope of attaining it honestly), and there is enough to crack the strongest youth. One study claimed that 84 percent of homeless youth suffered from depression. One fourth of those in a survey of Chicago homeless shelters said they felt sad and lonely most of the time.

Mental disease may take many forms. A teenage girl named Peggy fled her family on the West Coast to stay with an aunt in suburban Chicago. She was a well-behaved, model girl with the aunt. The aunt's husband, however, was not interested in keeping the girl. He talked about sending her back home.

Before long, Peggy began losing her vision. She needed to place a paper up against her face in order to read it. The stress of being a "perfect girl," so that she could stay with her aunt, was making her psychologically blind. Finally, she admitted that her father had molested her. She did not return to her parents.

Runaways, even when they seek health services, often have problems obtaining them. Most lack health insurance. All facilities except free clinics are off-limits to them. Even when they can receive services, many runaways avoid the health centers. They distrust most adults, especially those who might help force them back to their parents.

Even runaway shelters often sidestep the young people's medical care. Many of them do not even include questions about health on their intake forms. A 1990 study examined youth in federally funded shelters during 1989. Only 4 percent of them received or were referred to medical services. Less than 4 percent received drug or alcohol treatment. Only one sixth of those seen by shelter workers received any kind of medical care.

RUNAWAYS AND THE LAW

Runaways have more to worry about than food and shelter. Often they find the law is against them as well. At best, minors (including runaways) are second-class citizens. They lack many of the basic rights available to adults. They cannot work legally without permits, which parents must sign. Some schools will not allow minors to enroll without parental approval. Many doctors will not treat them, because of possible legal problems. Most cannot rent hotel or apartment rooms. Driver's licenses are almost impossible to obtain without a parental signature. They are restricted by numerous state and local curfews.

Minors are also subject to status offenses. These are laws which do not apply to adults but limit the rights of minors. They include laws against disorderly conduct, hitchhiking, and underage drinking. Leaving home without permission, refusing to obey parental rules, using vulgar language in public, having sex—all are classified as status offenses.

Status offenses account for most arrests of runaways. These arrests can lead to even greater nightmares for runaways. Status offenders, who generally commit victimless crimes, are sometimes incarcerated with adult criminals or juveniles who committed more serious crimes.

Even walking along the street can be risky. Police in many states have the right to take a child into custody if he or she is believed to be a runaway.

These laws are designed to serve three main purposes: to protect teenagers from themselves, to protect them from others, and to protect others from them. But instead of helping young people, status offenses often hinder them.

Herbert W. Beaver, author of *The Legal Status of Runaway Children*, wrote, "While not specifically so expressed, [status offenses] sometimes seem to carry with them an implied presumption against the child and seemingly place on the child the burden of proving that his running away was justified, without specifically spelling out what would constitute legally justifiable grounds for a child leaving home."

Laws may seem to favor parents over minors. A parent can petition juvenile courts to have a teenager declared incorrigible and placed into custody. Teenagers cannot do the same to incompetent parents.

The laws also tend to view all runaways in the same light. A bored kid on the road for kicks is considered the same as a child afraid to show the parents a bad report card or one fearing for his or her life because of past physical or sexual abuse.

Runaway laws are often vague and can vary from state to state. In fact, no clear definition of "runaway" exists. Some states make specific references in their laws to runaways; others do not. Some states allow chronic runaways to be institutionalized. Others place runaways under an "omnibus" clause, allowing the courts to do with them as they see fit. Many states have interstate compacts,

Runaways are most frequently arrested for status offenses. These are laws, such as curfews or bans on underage drinking, that limit the rights of minors.

allowing the arresting state to return the young offender to the state he or she originally fled.

Most runaways have little love for the courts. After all, the courts often gave them back to abusive parents, turned them over to uncaring foster parents, or threw them into the youthful equivalent of jails. They fit the runaway with labels like PINS (person in need of supervision), MINS (minor in need of supervision), or CHINS (child in need of supervision). For a young person, courts may be annoying, irritating, threatening or demeaning.

The judge is not viewed as a wise figure who gives rulings based on years of legal study and experience. That black-robed figure is merely another adult who is acting in the adults' interest against the youth. Some runaways left their biological or foster parents in part because of their dislike of the court system.

But many runaways never make it to the courts. While laws are on the books, many police have higher priorities than picking up runaways. If they do, life becomes even more unpleasant for the runaway than it was before. Former runaways comprise most of the youth population of detention centers, substance abuse centers, reform schools, and mental hospitals.

RUNAWAY STAGES

As runaways gain time and experience on the street or road, their lives and attitudes evolve. Things and people that were once of prime importance fade into the background, while persons or situations undreamed of weeks or months earlier take on new importance and significance.

Author Joseph E. Palenoski, in his book *Kids Who Run Away*, described three stages of runaway life: the unsettling stage, the exploratory stage, and the routinization stage. Successful runaways evolve through all three stages. Those who cannot handle the first two stages usually return home.

Runaways first on the road are in the unsettling stage. They think of themselves as persons away from home, not persons on the road. Their thoughts and actions are still very much home-centered. Often, their longing for home postpones the learning of basic runaway skills.

Those in the exploratory stage have overcome their initial fears and homesickness. They are interested in checking out the new world around them. While not totally familiar with their new surroundings, they show increasing interest in becoming part of them. As they become more comfortable, they conversely start flowing away from their former friends and lifestyles.

At this point, they start making changes that show commitment to their newly chosen existence. Their old friends' homes, where they might have slept since they left their parents, now seem too confining. They may leave for a cheap hotel or apartment.

Those who have reached the routinization stage are now veterans of the runaway trails. They are not observers of the runaway structure, but part of it. They rely on themselves, new friends, and institutions they have discovered during their time on the run. They have a routine and maybe a job. Runners in the routinization stage serve as models for the newer runaways.

Young people in the three stages have very different feelings about aspects of their lives:

Family contacts. Unsettling stage runaways still see their families as a major focus of their lives, even if they are no longer staying with them. Bad times and good times as well are magnified in the runaways' mind. Contacts with families may bring about a number of strong emotions, including depression. Those in the exploratory stage find contacts to be increasingly aggressive. A runaway at this stage realizes he or she no longer needs the family for his or her survival. By the time a runaway reaches the routinization stage, family contacts are infrequent or perhaps have ceased altogether.

Location or residence. Those in the unsettling stage are still home-based. They may be staying within blocks, or perhaps a few miles, of their parents. In many cases, they pay attention to the local grapevine to find out news of their families. If a sudden change occurs (a family member appears to have a change of heart, or someone suddenly becomes ill), they may scurry back home. Friend-based relationships are the keystone of those in the exploratory stage. These friends sometimes provide a smooth transition between the runaway's previous world and the independence they need in order to survive on the outside. Those who have reached the routinization stage have gone beyond their old friends. They have become independent or have encountered a circle of friends removed from their earlier world.

Perception of court. Runaways in the unsettling stage still see the court as a threat. The court, after all, took them from their parents, stuck them with some unfeeling foster parents, or threw them into a penal institution. For those in this group, courts are something to be avoided. The courts still can be an irritant to those in the exploratory stage, but by this time the skilled runaway has had plenty of experience avoiding them. When a runaway gets to the routinization stage, the attitude becomes one of indifference. He or she no longer thinks of the court, and usually the legal system all but gives up looking for him or her.

Friendship network. Those in the unsettling stage still look toward home for their main friendships. These are the people the runaway grew up with, who know his or her fears and dreams. If the runaway experience fails quickly, they may return home to their old pals. These longtime friends may still play a role to those in the exploratory stage, but that role decreases every day. Runaways in the routinization stage have completely transferred their alliance to a new social group. At most, one or two friends from the old days remain. They stand as living relics from the past, rather than as active friends from the runaway's day-to-day life.

School concerns. The longer away from school, the lower a priority it has. School is still on the mind of the newly loose young people in the unsettling stage. The joys of the school still bring nostalgia—or, more likely, the scars of the unpleasant school experience still evoke bitterness and sadness. When a runaway gets to the exploratory stage, he or she is no longer committed to the former school. It was not something that was good or bad. It was just something that happened, like many other factors of the previous life. By the time a runaway attains the routinization stage, school might as well never have happened.

Skills. How well can a young person live on the streets or the roads, by him- or herself? The skills of runaways in the unsettling stage are untested. They soon learn the answer and stay out or return home accordingly. The skills of those in the exploratory stage are constantly expanding. By now, they have shown themselves and others that they can survive away from home if they so desire. If they decide to stay away from home long enough, they reach the routinization stage. Younger and less experienced runaways pattern themselves after these savvy veterans.

VICTIMS AND VICTIMIZERS

Who are runaways? Many are victims of almost any kind of abuse that society can offer. They are held up, robbed, beaten, shot full of drugs, or forced to sell their bodies and pose for pornographic pictures. They talk of incest, rape, and violence as casually as other teenagers talk about dates or basketball games.

They may be victims, but they are not always innocent ones. Many beat up other people, steal, con, deal drugs, panhandle, join gangs, hustle, and strip in sleazy nightclubs.

Tom, a Los Angeles runaway, was one such victimizer. He robbed people and held up stores, often while under the influence of drugs. Tom showed no pity for his victims. Thinking about them only put him in a bad mood.

Aggressive criminals are a minority, according to Margi Dechenner, director of a Portland emergency shelter. "I'm sure that some street kids do commit crime," she said, "but they're the victims first. Real street kids have a belief system and strong sense of loyalty. It's very moving to see how much they'll sacrifice for the ones they love."

Many runaways view their lives as attack or be attacked. John, a San Francisco runaway, commented, "It's like you gotta be strong all the time, and always looking out for everybody, because everybody wants to hurt you somehow." Stephen Tarkelson, a worker at New York's Covenant House, added, "If you live on the streets for more than one to three months, you've got to be abused, and you've got to abuse people."

Former U.S. Senator Birch Bayh, who sponsored a major law to aid runaways, described their vulnerability. "The children who run look for companionship, friendship, and approval from those they meet," he said. "Many such youth are easy marks for gangs, drug pushers, and pimps."

Linda was one such runaway. Although she was very close to her father, she was placed in her mother's custody during a divorce settlement. Linda fled her mother and stayed with a married couple. Instead of being helpful, they forced her into prostitution. Linda sneaked a message to neighbors so that they would notify the police. The neighbors, however, told her captors. They beat her and left her for dead outside of town.

Later, Linda evaluated her experience. She said that running away "is a neat idea when you're about to leave. But when you get out there, things are different. You can't depend on anyone. When you run away, it's like getting on your knees and letting anybody walk by and slap you."

They may escape one type of harm by leaving home, but runaways often trade one hell for another. Living in neighborhoods where only the menacing and menaced survive, runaways cope by deadening themselves to the environment. Their living conditions take their physical and mental toll. "You can literally watch them age, week by week," said San Francisco shelter official Roger Hernandez.

Runaways soon lose another youthful quality—their innocence. Of all the things the streets take away from a youth, this might be the most painful. Terri, a Los Angeles shelter resident, said, "After living on the streets, I'll never be able to trust anybody again. Whenever anyone says they'll do something for me, I just think of what they're gonna want in return. I don't trust nobody. Everybody wants something from you. I'm only 16 now, but I'm no kid. I wish I could be, but I can't."

Almost all runaways who can leave the life sooner or later. A Portland, Oregon, security guard noted, "They get off because of the potential for violence. The ones that don't were so badly abused as children that they have no idea how to assimilate into society."

Bettina escaped the runaway life. Looking back, she explained, "I learned some things [while living on a Los Angeles beach]: humility, street smarts, different values—and I'm glad I have them. I just wished I would have learned them some other way."

CULTS

A tired, hungry, frightened, depressed runaway may just about give up hope when someone comes to cheer him or her up. This someone may offer happiness and flattery that are alien to the runaway's current life, then invite the youngster to meet other friends. These "friends" bombard the unsuspecting runaway with companionship if he or she stays with the group. They may promise a happy extended family, living and working together for a noble goal. Before long, a newly brainwashed convert may end up as a helpless or hopeless member of a cult.

In years past, cults were obvious and sometimes colorful parts of a city scene. On one street corner might be tamborine- and drum playing beggars dressed in the saffron robes of Buddhist monks. Across the street, one could find a black-cloaked person hawking books from another "religious" group. Modern cults are less visible than these earlier groups. They are more sophisticated.

There are many varieties of cults. There are religious cults and semireligious New Age cults. Fringe political groups may take on the nature of cults. Some cults disguise themselves as therapy or self-awareness groups. Others practice satanism or ritual abuse. Some have lasted for decades, while the life span of others

Cults may seem to offer a safe haven to a lonely, frightened, and hungry runaway. The haven can become a trap. Young people need to be aware of the motives and methods behind these groups.

is only as long as that of their founders. Some cults vanish quietly. Others, like David Koresh's Branch Davidian Temple (which ended in a fireball of gunfire and explosions) or Jim Jones's People's Temple (where more than 900 members drank poison in a South American jungle) perish in a storm of publicity.

Generally, cults avoid trying to recruit teenage runaways. Many groups search out college students or young adults, people with more access to money than the average runaway. Also, many groups fear the possible legal charges of kidnapping a minor. However, some runaways encounter these groups, and young people should be aware of their motives and methods.

Whether cults are religious, political, commercial or psychological in nature, they have some common elements. These include:

Mind control. Cult members will try to force someone to accept their views without criticism, discussion, or thought. New recruits are worn down by techniques such as massive group pressure, separation from the outside world, sleep deprivation, inadequate nutrition, and use of fear and guilt.

Charismatic leadership. One individual or a small group of leaders claim special knowledge, which they do not share freely with the general members of the group.

Deception. Cults recruit new members or solicit funds without being open or honest about their real goals.

Alienation. Cults demand that recruits separate themselves from family, friends, and past experiences—in short, their previous lives. Contact with family or previous friends is prevented or severely limited. Cults present a black-and-white view of the world—"we" are right and "they" (everyone who is not part of our group) are wrong.

Over a period of time, cults can bring about a number of harmful effects to their members. These include loss of free will, development of dependency upon the leader and his (cult leaders are usually male) henchmen, loss of spontaneity or sense of humor, inability to form friendships outside the cult, physical deterioration, and exploitation. Cult members have been coerced into working long hours begging or selling knickknacks for money that they turn over to the cult—conditions little better than slavery.

What should you do if a friend or relative becomes involved with a cult? Record names, addresses, and telephone numbers of suspected cult members. Answer communications from the friend or relative in a friendly and noncritical manner. Do not send money to the individual, as that money is likely to be passed directly to the cult. Above all, seek help from the Cult Awareness Network or other established groups that have knowledge of and experience in dealing with cults.

SUICIDE AND DEATH

For some runaways, the ultimate danger awaits. They may kill themselves, or someone else may kill them. Running away may actually prevent some suicides. For some young people, flight is a safety valve. They might commit suicide if they stayed home. Other kids almost use running as a suicidal gesture. They have a death wish, and they allow the streets to take them.

Juvenile suicides tripled during the 1970s. An estimated thirty youngsters took their lives daily. Many of those suicides were runaway youth.

Unfortunately, these deaths often go unnoticed and unmourned. Many, while on the run, remained anonymous by choice. Runaways seldom carry identification. Their families, many of which threw them out of the home, fail to notify police of their absence. Some 5,000 teenagers each year are buried in unmarked graves.

Johnny, in Los Angeles, said, "The place is large, and they can vanish here and not be found. What they forget is that there can be a danger, too. Young guys have been known just to vanish. Some poor kid comes running to L.A., gets picked up by someone offering help, and ends up being tortured to death so some weirdos can have their fun."

"Today it's a lot more dangerous on the streets than it was a few years ago," commented James, another Los Angeles runaway. "Stay home and train your mind instead of going out trying to be bad on the streets and getting yourself killed."

3

MAKING A LIVING

I had thirty-five dollars of money that I'd saved up from babysitting for my sisters and everybody. I figured, well . . . I have enough to support me until eternity.
—Gene, a San Francisco runaway

The adventure and excitement ends early. A young person on the road who has not given up and returned home must start working to survive on the streets.

Runaways soon learn a fearsome reality of life: It takes money to survive. Even those who stay with friends or relatives or are "kept" by strangers need money to buy life's luxuries. The rest need money just to buy most of its necessities.

Honest jobs that pay a living wage are not that easy to find. Some industrious or lucky runaways find such jobs. The rest live an existence that is not so easy or so honorable. This often means engaging in activities many would never dream of doing at home.

Most runaways leave home with little money and few possessions. The money usually goes faster than they had planned, and possessions may also depart, either from theft or from sale at a price far below their market value. Since most runaways (especially younger ones) possess few skills for legitimate jobs, they have one "asset" left—their bodies.

Young runaways—male as well as female—engage in survival sex, trading themselves for

With no money, no education, and no skills, runaways often end up selling the only thing they have—themselves. They work as juvenile prostitutes or as child performers in sex shows and pornographic films.

money or other favors so they can survive. Survival sex usually takes the form of prostitution. Runaways may go to Times Square in New York City or Market Street in San Francisco. In Los Angeles, girls solicit on Sunset Strip while boys ply their trade on Santa Monica Boulevard.

One section of New York's Eighth Avenue is called the "Minnesota strip." It got the name because pimps went to Minnesota to lure the young blonde girls that some of their clients preferred. The pimps sometimes promised modeling jobs, but the girls ended up with an entirely different type of work.

Nearly all juvenile prostitutes are runaways or throwaways. But few runaways leave home with the intention of becoming prostitutes (although some have sold themselves before making their first run). Some teens, however, head to a city even while realizing that prostitution may soon be a necessity.

Most long-term runaways, willing or not, peddle sex sooner or later. One study determined that 54 percent of runaways became prostitutes. Boys as well as girls are involved. There may be as many as 300,000 young male prostitutes on the streets in the United States. Many, if not most, of these male hustlers do not consider themselves homosexual. Prostitution to them is a necessary business, not sexual pleasure.

Why do runaways turn to prostitution? Is it because they are so ashamed of themselves that they give away their last bit of self-pride? For most, noted Rev. Lee Lowrey of Chicago's Night Ministry, the reason is simple. "After a couple of weeks on the streets and you don't have any cash, you sell yourself," he said. "When you get hungry, your self-esteem gets put on the back burner." Father Ritter added, "When you're 14 or 15 and you can't read or write very well, and you have no place to live, and it's cold and you're hungry, and you have no marketable skills, you market yourself."

At first, the money to be made from performing sex acts can be a lure. Ally, a Los Angeles runaway, was walking along a street with a friend when they encountered a prostitute. She told them, "Why give sex away when you can make money from it?" That notion made sense to the girls, and soon they started the work themselves.

Runaways with a history of incest or other sexual abuse may turn to prostitution. They have learned first-hand that sex is not always a loving act. If they can't get love from sex, they might as well get profit.

Performing sex acts pays a lot more money than flipping burgers—when the prostitute is allowed to keep the money that he or she earns. That is not always the case.

Sometimes, the road to prostitution starts less than five minutes after a kid enters a city. Frightened, confused youths are easy targets for pimps who create and then prey on prostitutes.

Many pimps steer clear of underage girls or boys. Judges tend to give stiff sentences to pimps who deal with minors. Young people are also less predictable and trustworthy than older ones. However, youngsters may be easily frightened or threatened. Besides, many perverted adults take bizarre satisfaction from sex with children.

"Some flashy pimp with a big fancy Cadillac comes up," said Brad Bailey, a Portland, Oregon policeman. "The kid has never gotten attention. The guy starts talking to her, she makes the decision right then and there. 'I'll go with this guy and hopefully it will make life easier.'"

The pimp may show up pretending to be the friend the runaway never had back home. Are you hungry? He springs for a free meal. Need a place to stay? He just so happens to have a spare room. Want to get high? The pimp manages to have access to marijuana or stronger drugs. Want to meet some nice kids? This adult seems to have a number of teenage "friends."

Pimps may sweet-talk young people to them. But often they use decoys to lure unsuspecting youths. Many young people may be leery of a flashy dude driving around in a gaudy automobile. But that friendly middle-aged (or pregnant) woman can't be harmful, can she? That woman also happens to have an apartment with lots of food and a spare room. After a short time, she introduces a male "friend" to the runaway.

Sometimes, the process is gradual. The kid hangs around the pimp's apartment a few days, relaxing and enjoying the good life. Then reality strikes. By the way, hints the pimp, there is something you can do to show your gratitude. Within a matter of days or weeks, an innocent or frightened small-town girl may take on the look of a hardened streetwalker.

At other times, reality sets in much faster. In the nineteenth century, immigrant girls were kidnapped and repeatedly assaulted by professional rapists until they agreed to prostitution. Even today, such practices endure. A girl named Jeannie was drugged and raped repeatedly for a week. She escaped to a New York shelter. The next day, her pimp showed up at the shelter, demanding "his" girl back. It was no surprise that the pimp wanted her. After all, the girl could bring three thousand dollars a month, tax-free, to him.

"It was strange at first, but I got used to it—I had to," said Terry, a Los Angeles runaway. "I just took off my clothes and did what the guy wanted. I'd take about forty or fifty bucks, do what I had to do, then give the money to Lamar [her pimp]. I didn't get nothin' . . . the only thing he did for me was get me pot . . . I just sat there all day and got high with his other girls. . . . There was one little girl . . . I think she was ten. I wanted to talk to her, but I was too scared. She tried to run away and Lamar was beatin' up on her. She was a runaway, too."

Fourteen-year-old Jennifer, whose father tried to molest her, fled to New York. She met a man who offered to talk with her father. The kindly stranger turned out to be a pimp. He raped her and put her to work on the streets.

One day he took her to a hotel where he had customers waiting. She eluded him and hid in a bathroom for three hours. She then found a hotel securi-

Street kids have to grow up fast. They are at constant risk of becoming victims of violence, rape, and sexually transmitted diseases.

ty guard, who contacted the police. Jennifer returned home.

Boys also may be trapped into working for pimps. Don, a 14-year-old, was forced into prostitution in New York. He was tied to a bed for four days and raped seventeen times. The rapist later confessed, "The kid resisted at first, so we beat him and, just to teach him a lesson, burned his back with a cigarette."

"I lived with fourteen other boys in this big house," recalled Mark, another prostitute. "We were all pretty young, and pretty scared. [Our pimp] made all of us watch a kid getting beaten with a hanger. It was bad. That's what happened when you tried to leave. Next time, you're dead."

Many prostitutes of both sexes first got involved through child pornography. While a kid may at first not be willing to perform sex acts with strangers, it is easy to pose naked in front of a camera. From there, he or she may have sex in a studio with acquaintances. Once resistance to performing commercial sex is broken, it is an easy step to the streets.

Amazingly, child pornography is legal in some places. In New York state, persons aged 16 and over are no longer considered runaways. Instead, they are classified as homeless people. It is virtually impossible for 16-year-olds without a high school diploma to find a decent job. They cannot legally register in a hotel. They are too young to drink, vote, or serve in the military. They cannot legally watch X-rated films. But they can star in those films.

Boy prostitutes are more likely to work independently (without pimps) than girls. They are less likely to be arrested than are the girls, perhaps because male police officers are more willing to pose as heterosexual customers than homosexual ones.

Even those prostitutes not involved with pimps dislike the work. "Working the streets is degrading. I know I was being used," commented Benny, a Los Angeles prostitute.

Often, they feel they have no option. Jim, a New York runaway, confessed, "I've got two choices. I can go with a john and sell my tail, or I can rip somebody off and go to jail. And I'm afraid to go to jail. I wouldn't make it through my first shower [without being raped]."

A study by San Francisco's Huckleberry House shelter confirmed that teens felt prostitution was a necessity. Eighty-five percent of male prostitutes, said the study, started "when they were on the run, broke, and needed money for food and shelter."

Most teenage prostitutes have little regard for their johns. Christine, a teenager from Kentucky, fled to Los Angeles. Her first trick (prostitution job) involved a middle-aged man. She was too nervous to discuss money with him. Instead, she began crying. The startled man threw her some money and left. "It was like he was really, really embarrassed," she said later. "He was older than my father even."

Vikki, a Seattle runaway, said "I think it's very strange that older men like little girls because they're perverts, that's what it is. I mean, I like the money, but I don't like them."

Some runaways can spot a potential prostitution situation and leave before it is forced upon them. Cindi, a 16-year-old, recalled, "I was living with this guy, we liked each other and he wasn't too old. . . . One time he says I got to help his 'club,' and that I need to be there on Friday nights. I said okay, but when I was there, people start grabbing your body . . . so everybody thinks it's fun but you . . . I ain't living there no more and I'm glad; it ain't worth the hassle. If he thinks I'm going to be in that kind of business . . . no way!"

Runaways who have avoided or quit prostitution often criticize those who continue. Seattle runaway Randi commented, "Most of the kids on the streets, that's how they survive. They feel like if they don't do the dates they're gonna be broke, they're gonna have to Dumpster-dive, they're gonna have to beg for money, and . . . they're gonna feel like 'I'm no good, I'm dirty, I'm rotten, I'm scum, I'm livin' in this rathole [with] no water, no electricity, no nothin' . . . I'm beggin' money.' I guess they feel that's worse than pullin' dates. I don't know what their problem is."

Los Angeles runaway Ally, herself a former prostitute, sympathized with those still working the streets. "I feel sorry for all the girls—and guys, too—who have to turn tricks to survive," she said. "It's a terrible thing to do. But it works, you know, and it's not easy to leave it behind when you know how easily you can make a lot of money."

The "world's oldest profession" may put dollars in the pocketbook for the short run, but it takes years from your life in the long run. Prostitutes, because of the degrading nature of their work, risk a variety of problems. Communicable diseases are always a threat. They are prime candidates for psychological problems such as drug abuse, depression, and suicide.

Most young prostitutes' careers don't last long. They face an unstoppable enemy—time. The childish cuteness that makes teenagers attractive to many johns is lost before long. For most runaways, the strains of living on the streets only accelerates the aging process.

Violence is a way of life for many prostitutes. Billy Jo, a Portland runaway, noted the street "is not the place to be. I was raped several times down here. . . . Yeah, it's not all fun and games."

Prostitution can be a gamble for both hustler and customer. For either, their next enounter could be the fatal one. Most teenage prostitutes do not lead high-profile lives. They seldom carry identification. They may not be known to anyone except fellow prostitutes. Even then, they may be only known by nickname. If they suddenly disappear by foul play, who notices?

"You know you always hear those stories about men who pay a hustler to come home with them and then get beaten and robbed. Well, it's true. That does happen," admitted Johnny, a Los Angeles runaway and hustler. "But it's also dangerous to hustle. A guy vanishes. He has no friends. Landlord thinks he split to avoid paying the rent. And nobody does anything. A few months later an unidentified body is found in the Valley somewhere."

"You don't know if you're going to be shot, stabbed, or taken to Mexico," said Billy, another Los Angeles street hustler. Vikki, the Seattle street kid, adds, "You can get beat up, and some of these [prostitutes] end up getting killed."

Veronica was 10 years old when she brought her friend Diana to her suburban New York home. Diana wanted Veronica to visit her in Manhattan. Veronica's parents refused. Days later, Veronica made her first run from home.

When the school year began, she vanished for a month. Then came news of her arrest for prostitution. Veronica returned to school, but her behavior changed. Veronica had always worn jeans to school. Now it was makeup, jewelry, and high heels—when she decided to attend school. She spent more time working on Manhattan's Minnesota strip than she spent studying.

Her prostitution career ended suddenly one summer evening. Her body cracked as it hit the sidewalk pavement. Veronica fell, jumped, or was pushed from a tenth-story window.

DRUG DEALING

Prostitution is not the only illegal activity used by runaways to gain money. A high percentage of runaways have admitted to selling drugs for quick cash. Often, the drug dealers are former prostitutes. "What else are you going to do when you're too old to make it on the street?" asked a New York runaway. "When you can't find a job and a place to live? After you grow a beard and nobody will buy you? What else can you do besides steal and deal drugs?"

The drug subculture may appear to be very glamourous to a young person living alone on the street.

Throwaways particularly engage in drug dealing. Their behavior at home often included using or selling drugs. Sometimes, the drugs were the reason their parents discarded them. "You get a lot of kids with substance abuse problems and the parents can't deal with it and so they put them out," said Brad Ferguson, a detective in suburban Chicago.

Now that they are on the street and with no chance of returning home, these drug dealers have nothing to lose by engaging in illegal activity. Their position on the fringe of society makes it easy for them to meet current and potential drug users.

Perhaps the most common method of securing drugs is through prescriptions. A runaway gets prescriptions from willing doctors, fills them at a local pharmacy, then sells them at a profit.

Kelli was one such drug merchant. The 16-year-old girl traded sex for prescriptions. To her, sex was strictly business. Then she sold the pills to connections in the neighborhood and at local schools.

Wendell, a Chicagoan, went from poverty to running away and selling drugs. He said, "We never had enough food. I knew what to do. I told [my parents] I'd see them later. . . . I slept in vacant apartments for two or three weeks . . . But I couldn't keep enough food in my mouth so I approached getting money in the wrong manner—I started selling dope."

Selling drugs is another way to make quick money on the streets, but the risk of violence and arrest is just as great as that faced by prostitutes.

The police eventually caught up to Wendell. They arrested him for two counts of selling drugs. "I worry about getting locked up," he confessed. "I worry about my youngest brother getting into trouble like me. And I worry about myself—how to live my life."

THEFT, PANHANDLING, AND CON GAMES

As the numbers of runaways increase, so does juvenile crime. Because honest work is not available, many runaways turn to delinquent behavior. When all else fails, many runaways resort to theft. This may involve shoplifting, conning credit from local stores, or even burglary.

"I stole everything from every kind of store you can think of—drug stores, supermarkets, all of them," Los Angeles runaway Terry recalled. "I'd walk into the market with one of those big beach baskets, and I'd walk out with ten cartons of cigarettes inside . . . I'd stuff anything in my basket: clothes, make-up, even a radio one time."

Most young thieves work alone, although some team up with partners. One distracts the victim, while the other lifts the desired goods. Food is the most common item stolen, although anything is fair game. Sometimes young people will take expensive items from stores and later try to return them for refunds.

Authorities take a dim view of juvenile theft, whether the person is a runaway or not. For both males and females, the first criminal conviction is usually for shoplifting. Since this is usually considered to be a "victimless" crime, the young offender is often released. After the first offense, the runaway is usually returned home. Most are even returned after the second offense, although females are more likely to be detained. By the time of the third arrest, young offenders might graduate from petty theft to more serious crimes, such as burglary or larceny. These offenders almost always spend some time behind bars.

Sometimes, instead of outright taking money or goods, runaways will try to persuade others into giving them willingly. Their small-time confidence games are often less than sophisticated. The results are not always what the runaway wants.

Patrick, a Los Angeles resident, described how a scam could backfire when he pretended his car was out of gas. "Another guy from the squat, and two girls I knew from the street would drive down the road, pull over to the side, and pretend the car had broken down," he said. "Me and the guy would get out and start pushing, and the girls would stay in the front seat. . . . It was great because me and one of the girls were black and the other two were white—we had all the racial percentages covered.

"There were some people . . . who said, 'Here, I'll buy you a little gas on my credit card. . . . That really [irritated] us, you know. We didn't

DUMPSTER-DIVING

Runaways have to eat, just like anyone else. Even when money for food is not available, there are several ways they get dinner. Most are illegal, and all are frowned upon by restaurant owners.

Some runaways get meals by "table scoring," snatching up unattended food before it is thrown away. "Dash and dive," eating at a restaurant and running out without paying, is another trick. Jack, a Seattle runaway, said, "You go into a restaurant, you know. You order something. Usually they'll sit you right by the cash register if you look young, like you don't have no money, so they can see you. But right by the cash register is right by the door, so it works out better."

"Dumpster-diving" provides regular food for some runaways. "You call for a pizza and give your number over a pay phone," said Jack. "They make the pizza, nobody claims it, they throw it into the Dumpster, and you get it."

Some runaways claim particular Dumpsters as part of their turf. "When you get a regular Dumpster, we call them regs, you know you go there every night . . . you can tell, because they're regs, what was there last week and what was put in that night," claimed Jack. "A lot of people say that stuff's been in there a week, but you can tell, 'cause that's your regular Dumpster."

really need gas—that we could always siphon off from another car. We needed cash for drugs."

The more a runaway practices a particular confidence game, the better he or she becomes at it. At the same time, the more frequently the scam is worked, the greater chance the person has of being arrested.

Less ambitious than the thieves and the confidence artists are the panhandlers. They beg on the streets, hoping to catch passersby in a generous mood.

Panhandlers are more visible than thieves or con artists. Often they arouse opposition from local neighbors or merchants. A sign in Chicago's Lakeview neighborhood notes that panhandling is against the law. "Please don't help people to break our laws. If you see anyone [panhandling], please report them to the police," the sign reads.

The simplest form of panhandling is "spainging," directly asking strangers for spare change. Veterans of the street have this form of moneymaking down to a science. "I never panhandle during rush hour," noted Sunshine, a Chicago street person. "The people who work normal jobs and get off the bus or train just walk by and pretend you're not there."

Dan, a Chicago runaway, commented, "I was spainging for drugs the other day. I got seven bucks in twenty minutes. I ask for food, they never give it to me. So now, I just spainge for drugs."

Minorities have a harder time panhandling than do white runaways. A panhandler must be able to approach potential customers without appearing threatening. Many white adults are apprehensive about minority youths asking for money. Prosperous minority adults may be no more generous.

Circumstances keep some begging. Ally, a Los Angeles girl, said, "I've been out on the streets panhandling once or twice, with some other kids from the shelter, and the tourists are always, like, 'Why don't you get a job?' I'm too young to get a job. 'Why don't you go back home where you belong?' Well, let's see. My mom beats me and my father molests me. What's at home?"

Some runaways never return to a regular life. They become permanent street people, and panhandling for small change becomes their life work. Most tire of begging. Sooner or later, they find something else to do. A Los Angeles girl named Green remarked, "What scares me is when I get older, I want to get married and have an apartment. I don't want to be panhandling."

HONEST WORK

Most runaways, if given the choice, would accept full-time work that pays them a living wage. Even the least-motivated idler perks up and changes all plans if he or she hears about a possible job. A job, even a temporary one, means money, independence, and an increased dose of self-respect.

There aren't many employment options available to underage teenagers who have left home. Begging may seem like the only choice, but it is illegal in many places.

Unfortunately for most runaways, several factors work against them. Most important is age. Youths under age 18, runaway or not, may find jobs that pay a minimum wage. Work that pays more than that is extremely rare. As for those under age 16—forget it.

Being asked for identification by a would-be employer poses another problem. Many runaways harbor fears of discovery by police. An adult who knows their name and address might turn them in to the authorities and force them back to their parents. "Employers ask for honesty," said Andi, a Chicago runaway. "But a lot of kids here are on the run from the law. You can't get a job for fear of being sent to the Audy Home [a juvenile detention center] or a psych ward or an abusive home."

For most runaways, education is a problem. Employers generally want high school graduates for responsible jobs. Younger teens obviously don't have diplomas. Most older runaways also lack high school degrees. Likewise, they lack the work experience or skills some employers might accept in place of education.

If an employer hires a young person, it might be for cheap labor. Wages may seem reasonable at first, but once payroll deductions are made, the run-

Honest work is hard to find for runaways. Many are too young to work legally. Those who are old enough to work don't have the education or skills to get well-paying jobs.

away takes home a check much smaller than he or she hoped. Maintaining a decent standard of living can be more difficult than imagined.

Often, runaways lack discipline when it comes to attendance or showing up on time. These may be the bad habits which brought about problems at school and home. An undisciplined student is likely to become an undisciplined worker and may have difficulties holding on to a job. This lack of reliability by one runaway may affect future runaways as well. An employer who had a bad experience with a kid three weeks ago may not feel like hiring another.

Runaways also confront other obstacles that deter possible employment. Their status by itself works against them. Mike, a Los Angeles runaway, commented, "I actually got kicked out of a place where I was trying to get a job because I told a guy I was homeless and wanted to get on my feet."

Krista, another Los Angeles job-seeker, added "I get [angry] here when they tell me I can't do something here because I'm not an adult. I mean, I've been through all this stuff, but I still can't get any of the good jobs out there because I'm not an adult?"

Cleanliness is another worry. Someone living in a squat, unable to wash clothes or take a shower, may have a hard time making a good impression at a job interview.

Even those who are clean have appearances that may bother adults. "People are hiring, but you have to look a certain way," noted Sunshine, a Chicago runaway. "Kids out here just don't look like good little boys or girls," added Andi.

"I've gone into places with help wanted signs in the window, and I go and people look me over and see all my earrings and turn me down," said Andi. "Going by appearances is not fair to many people. For a lot of them, like Native Americans, tattoos are a ritual part of their religion."

Still, some jobs are available. Andi found work with an environmental group. "I filled out fifty-nine applications," she said. "I have motivation. I got dressed up and went to their office. I said, 'I'll do the first day's job for free.' So now I get up and go to work, and when the day's over, I feel like I've done something."

The average runaway probably will not find a job as good as the one Andi got. Some encounter short-term or part-time day labor jobs. They could work as dishwashers or bus tables. A few, if they can fool club owners, work as dancers or strippers. The work may be low-paying or demeaning. But every paycheck adds up to a little more time that a runaway can stay out on his or her own.

Despite their present conditions, most runaways still have dreams that they can escape their current lives. Some manage to hang on, perhaps gaining a high school equivalency certificate or joining the armed forces. Others never quite make it. And the longer they stay on the streets, the deeper the hole they dig for themselves.

4

HELP IS OUT THERE

You can tell them by their clean shoes and backpacks and that scared look on their faces.
—"Seven," a San Francisco outreach worker, describing newly arrived runaways at a bus station

For most runaways, the pressure of the streets will become too much to handle. There will be one too many ripoffs, one too many hungry or sleepless nights, one too many near-arrests, one too many bad experiences with johns or pimps.

As Diane, a street veteran, points out, "A lot of these kids run away from home looking for adventure and excitement, but that wears off real fast. Then the only thing left is survival, man, by whatever means you can find."

Fellow runaways cannot help. It becomes time to seek those with sufficient resources to help runaways. Fortunately, help is out there.

Many runaways use runaway shelters as their first formal link to adults while on the streets. The shelters are what their name implies—places of safety where youths can temporarily escape the pressures of the outside.

San Francisco's Huckleberry House was the first runaway house in the United States. It opened in 1967 during the "summer of love." Middle- to upper-class white hippies were the first customers. Now Huckleberry, like many big-city shelters, serves a largely minority population.

Runaway shelters provide homeless youths with a safe place to stay, food, counseling, and a chance to get their lives back together.

The Runaway and Homeless Youth Act of 1974 provided federal funding for runaway shelters. To qualify, a shelter must be located in an area accessible to runaway and homeless youth. It must have a maximum capacity of twenty persons or less. The shelter must have adequate plans for contacting parents and providing living arrangements for the youths. It must develop an adequate plan for counseling the kids and their parents.

Government funds helped upgrade many shelters. Ragtag groups that started with a founder here and a couple of volunteers there could afford to hire professionals. Now runaway shelters employ social workers, youth workers, and support staff. Volunteers are welcomed, although employers screen them before allowing them into the shelter.

Bridge Over Troubled Waters in Boston, Portland's Outside-In, Huckleberry House in San Francisco, Chicago's Neon Street, Covenant House of New York—each of these centers has its own unique philosophy and system. But most runaway shelters have several factors in common.

The shelters, by law, are required to try to reunite the kids with their parents. Some demand parental permission before a child is allowed to stay. Huckleberry House makes a telephone call to the child's parents. The child is encouraged, but not required, to talk to the parents. If they cannot be reached by phone, a telegram is sent. If the parents do not give permission, Huckleberry will not admit the child.

A call home may be what some runaways need. Options House in Hollywood claimed that 40 percent of the youths it counseled reunited with their families. Covenant House has claimed that more than a third of the residents in some of its shelters eventually went home.

Whether or not the kids stay in the shelter, most provide some kind of services. A kid may get a free meal, for instance. Some Los Angeles runaways memorize the food schedules of shelters and move among them for two or three meals a day. The food varies. Often it is a compromise between the strictly healthy choices of many counselors and the fast-food preferences of runaways.

Many centers also give free legal or medical services. In some cases they offer psychological or sexual or substance abuse counseling. Runaway shelters may provide access to jobs or training programs. Some give away donated clothing. All offer a free ear to listen to the runaways' problems.

Perhaps the most important immediate offering is a bed. The shelter provides a welcome alternative to a squat, park bench, alley, all-night movie theater, or home of a stranger where sex is the price of lodging. Not all shelters can offer a roof over the head to all runaways. While New York's Covenant House has a policy of not turning away anyone, Portland's Greenhouse accepts only youngsters that staff have dealt with previously. Some centers house only long-term runaways. They feel that the presence of short-term transients upsets the work they attempt with their regular clients.

Some runaway programs recognize that there isn't always a home to return to. These programs help teens finish high school and get proper job training so they can lead independent lives.

Girls more than boys tend to use shelters. Older runaways are more likely to stay in them than younger ones. For many residents, it is the second or third run from home. They know the ways of the streets, including where they can go for help.

Some youths use the shelter as a first step toward a planned return home. Others drop by from time to time, using the shelter as a rest from their regular activities. They enjoy life on the streets. To them, a shelter is just another source of support.

Prostitutes avail themselves of the shelter services. They might come in to escape a brutal pimp. Maybe they plan to give up the profession forever. At the least, they can grab a meal and a night's sleep without depending on a pimp or a patron.

Most runaways have good reason for using the shelters. "I seldom get a kid whom I feel is just a spoiled brat or someone who stomped off in a huff," said Sherri Pieros, a Huckleberry House worker.

Once inside the shelter, the youths may do a number of different things. Some programs insist that residents spend their days in counseling or looking for work or training. Others offer a more laid-back approach. The kids may hang around to recuperate and regain their physical and mental energies. They use this safe time to help plan their futures.

Counseling is one of the most important services available at runaway shelters. The counselors are often former runaways themselves.

A newsletter from Chicago's Night Ministry described a typical day at one of the Ministry's shelters: "The things kids do are the things that kids normally do . . . getting up as late as possible, getting ready for the day, eating breakfast, going off to work or school, arguing, doing laundry, and eating peach cobbler if it's around."

One of the main advantages of a shelter is the feeling of calm it can provide. After a time in a shelter, residents may begin to shed some of the suspicion they have of other people. Runaways can leave a shelter realizing that not everyone is a predator.

"Don't expect to get life stories from kids out of shelters. They're suspicious," noted Brian Love of the Night Ministry. In some cases, their fears and suspicions can be overwhelming. A Chicago social worker found a shelter for Mary, a runaway who had turned to prostitution and drugs. While she and the worker were waiting for a taxi to the shelter, Mary hid every time a police car passed. Had she been at some time a victim of police brutality? Was her fear an instinctive reaction from her days as a prostitute and drug user? The social worker had to keep reminding her, "We're just waiting for a cab. They can't arrest us for that."

Once runaways get over their fears, they can plan for the next phase of their lives. Is it time to return home? Is it possible to return home? Is it advisable to return home? Should I find my own apartment? Should I return to school? Are there alternative schools available? What kind of work can I get? Counselors at the shelter can help them make these difficult decisions.

The runaway centers offer definite advantages. Once inside, the young runner is assured of safety. Many runaway shelters hire security police. A runaway may find an immediate answer to a pressing food or health problem. Shelter workers will offer help, not sermons.

Yet many runaways stay away from the centers. First of all, if they want to stay at the shelter, they have to go by the center's rules. Some shelters have rules; others have "commitments." All have their own dos and don'ts. Alcohol, illegal drugs, weapons, and violence are forbidden. Residents are expected to be inside the shelter by a certain time each night. Some shelters admit both boys and girls, while others separate the sexes. In either case, sexual activity among residents is either outright forbidden or highly discouraged.

Runaways usually lack creature comforts. But on the streets, they come and go as they please. Many cannot handle adults telling them when they must be inside, or that they may not smoke or drink. For them, if they wanted rules, they could have stayed at home.

"You can go in them at first and rap and get help . . . but the people expect you to take a good look at yourself," claimed Robert, who stayed at shelters in southern California. "You're gonna have to let the people see that you are trying to help yourself. You need to play by the rules, keep or find some work. . . . You can't go running around all night. There are house rules you need to obey if you want to stay around and be helped."

Runaways often stay away from the shelters because they cannot stand up to the challenges there. Many runaway counselors are former runaways themselves. These veterans of the streets know the lies, the scams, and the self-deceptions that runaways use. It is difficult, if not impossible, to con them. These counselors do what many runaways hate—force them to examine their reasons for running and what they plan to do with themselves.

There are other problems. Some runaway centers are located away from downtown areas where young people gather. Despite promises from shelter workers, many runaways fear they will be turned over to law-enforcement authorities. Some kids just think they can make it on their own without the outside help of adults.

Most important, runaway shelters can provide only short-term solutions. Almost all shelters impose time limits on their residents. After a few weeks or a few months, they must go. The teen who enters a shelter with an alcohol or drug addiction or a school hassle or an abusive parent is likely to leave the center with his or her problem unresolved.

COVENANT HOUSE

In the 1960s, Father Bruce Ritter gave up a comfortable lifestyle as a teaching priest for active service in Manhattan's poverty-stricken Lower East Side. Moved by the plight of exploited runaways, Ritter let some stay with him. Soon, his apartment was bursting with runaway youngsters.

Ritter enlisted the help of anyone and everyone. The result of his effort is Covenant House, now the largest system of runaway facilities in the United States. Covenant House has more than a dozen chapters—from New York City to Fort Lauderdale, Florida, to Hollywood, to Anchorage, Alaska, plus three in Latin America.

Programs vary from place to place, as needs vary. Los Angeles is a fierce gang city. Youngsters flee to Covenant House if hounded by gang members. Fort Lauderdale, a middle-class community, hosts a Covenant House with a very active family reunification program. Parents come in over weekends and attend family workshops to help solve problems. In New York, however, problems at home are usually so severe that reuniting the family (or even returning to the runaway's native community) is usually not a good idea.

The programs no longer wait for runaways to come to them. Covenant House outreach vans, armed with sandwiches, hot chocolate, clothing, counselors, and hope, pull up alongside street kids. They offer a bite to eat, an ear to listen, and a brief respite from the street pressures. The philosophy of these vans

Covenant House operates outreach vans, bringing food, counseling, health care, and other services directly to kids on the street.

is, "If a kid passes up our help tonight, maybe he'll remember us and our blue van next time. Because he can be sure we'll be back tomorrow."

Covenant House in 1994 served about 40,000 young runaways. They were helped by about 1,500 people, both paid professionals and volunteers. "They are wonderfully organized, the way they use volunteers," said Robert Browning, a former New York Covenant House volunteer. "They were kind of picky about who they'd let in as a volunteer. There was one long training session where they laid out what to do or not to do. For instance, there was no physical contact allowed, not even a friendly pat on the back. To many of those kids, their background was so geared to prostitution that any kind of touching was considered sexual."

"Most [runaways] needed something a lot harder to supply than just bed and food—a future," noted founder Ritter. Covenant House over the years has aimed to help provide that future. In addition to providing a place to stay, it offers job training. Students and staff prepare a future plan. It may involve a direct job, or job training, or high school, or a combination of the three. The New York Covenant House has an apartment program. Covenant House signs an apartment lease for young workers who otherwise could not secure their own place. If the young tenants keep up rent payments for a full year, Covenant House turns the lease over to them.

Still, the major focus of Covenant House is the emergency shelter. Kids on the average stay from one to three weeks. During that time they receive individual and group counseling, vocational and educational training, health care, and help toward securing employment and housing.

RUNAWAY HOTLINES

Face-to-face confrontations can be frightening. It takes a lot of nerve to walk inside a strange building and meet with unknown adults. Some runaways fear this possible crisis. Yet they yearn to leave their present street conditions.

For them, the answer may be a few coins and a telephone away. Runaway hotlines, both national and local, provide instant and anonymous service to those away from home.

Houston, Texas, became a murder capital in 1973. The world watched stunned as the bodies of more than twenty boys and young men were found. Three drifters were later charged with the killings. It was the worst known murder spree victimizing young people in American history.

Many of these young victims were believed to be runaways. Did they ever have a chance to escape their uncertain lives? Would their fate have been different if they had contact with home?

Runaway hotlines offer a variety of confidential services. They pass on messages to family and friends, help runaways find shelters and services, and provide a sympathetic ear in times of need.

These questions helped bring about Operation Peace of Mind, the first national runaway switchboard. Operation Peace of Mind began as a temporary measure. It was intended as a hotline to answer questions from parents around the country who feared their sons were among the slain Texas youth.

Soon it became obvious that a need existed for a permanent runaway call-in service. Operation Peace of Mind continued and grew. The service (now known as Runaway Hotline) now fields more than 10,000 calls per month. Some of these callers are runaways. Others are concerned parents or friends.

A year later, the National Runaway Switchboard began. The Chicago-based organization began after testimony that led to the Runaway Youth Act of 1974. It, too, handles calls from around the country.

Volunteers at these hotlines will not give empty "just-go-home-and-everything-will-be-fine" responses to callers. Each switchboard answerer receives weeks of training—instruction on what to say, how to say it, and what not to say. Runaway switchboard callers may be in fragile emotional states any-way. A misplaced remark could turn them off, and nothing is easier for them than hanging up the phone. A caller who hangs up may be lost forever.

Exact methods vary, but most switchboards use similar techniques. If a runaway calls, the volunteer takes a message. Only that exact message is relayed to the parent or interested party. The volunteer asks the runaway to call back later. If the parent has a message for the runaway, the volunteer gives it. All messages are confidential.

Runaway switchboards will also forward mail. Letters from parents or runaways can be sent to the switchboard. From there they go to the desired recipient, without parents learning the runaway's address. The switchboards may act as neutral third parties to negotiate between parents and runaways. They may even set up conference calls in case both sides want to speak with each other.

The switchboards also connect runaways with available services. When someone new to the area calls a switchboard, the volunteer can tell of local shelters, churches, social agencies, clinics or other groups which may help. The runaway can learn of nearby legal aid, free clinics, housing, drop-in centers, run-away shelters, Travelers Aid or Salvation Army offices.

If the switchboard worker determines that the caller is a throwaway, the call is handled differently. The worker tries to link the caller with a nearby social service agency and send him or her there directly.

These switchboards are not just for people who have already left home. A talk with a switchboard counselor may convince a would-be runaway that there are better alternatives to the streets. Covenant House's Nineline fielded more than 1.4 million calls in 1994. A 14-year-old girl might call because even though she tries to be good, she feels blamed by her family for all the problems at home. A 12-year-old might call after his father beat him with a belt for the third time in a week. A 13-year-old might think of running away because she was being terrified by a group of girls at school. A counselor can refer the callers to local agencies, set up conference calls with parents, or maybe just be the supportive person needed to hear someone's gripe.

National switchboards make themselves known through television and radio public service announcements and articles in national magazines and newspapers. They post notices in parks, libraries, bus stations, and other centers where young people might congregate.

Yet local switchboards may get more use than the national ones. Most runaways stay within a few miles of their home. They may know the local telephone answerers, and the local hotlines have the latest access to nearby facilities.

Hotlines serve only a small percentage of runaways. Many do not know they exist. Others do not understand the hotlines' confidentiality and fear that a telephone call may lead to their arrest.

SOCIAL SERVICE AGENCIES

One runaway girl described the perfect social service agency as "an empty house with a full fridge." In other words, she wanted all of the benefits an agency could provide without any adult intervention. That service does not exist. Many others do, however, including agencies little used by runaways.

These groups take many forms. They include Travelers Aid, crash pads, legal aid groups, free clinics, police services, hospitals, free food projects, church programs, drop-in centers, and drug abuse clinics.

Originally, the Travelers Aid Society served as an information center for people on the road. In recent years, it assumed more social service duties. Police will refer runaways to Travelers Aid, but Travelers Aid will not turn runaways over to the authorities. Travelers Aid helps runaways arrange transportation home or to shelters. Some bus companies cooperate by paying the fare of a runaway who wants to return home. However, few runaways know of or use Travelers Aid's services.

Crash pads offer the barest of necessities—a place to sleep, and maybe a bite for breakfast. Their name comes from hippie days, when people coming into a new town immediately searched for a place to "crash," or sleep. In some places, overnight warming shelters operate during the colder months.

Women's shelters help victims, adult or minor, who escape their homes to avoid physical or sexual abuse. Since husbands, fathers, or boyfriends of these women may become violent, the shelters operate under high confidentiality. Some of the shelters hire armed guards to prevent intruders. Women's shelters seldom accept visitors off the streets. But if they have room, they will take women referred by another agency.

NIGHT MINISTRY

"Sometimes all that's required is to be there—not always solving the problem, because many problems can't be solved. What's required is to care enough to share the pain of the moment."

That philosophy, given by Rev. Tom Behrens, is what started Chicago's Night Ministry, a unique program that hits the streets to help runaways and other street people.

Behrens realized that many people in need would not come to a social service agency. So the Night Ministry goes looking for them. It focuses on the streets, bars, and all-night restaurants where people in need gather. A Night Ministry worker may spend one evening in the largely gay and lesbian Broadway area, the next night in racially and culturally mixed Uptown, and the third night among the youth and runaways at Clark and Belmont. The walking ministers provide crisis intervention, informal counseling, referral to other services, friendship, and sometimes, a shoulder to cry on.

A 53-foot-long Health Outreach Program (HOP) bus brings more Night Ministry services to the streets. If nothing else, a street person can step inside to sip a cup of coffee and warm up on a cold Chicago night. For those who want it, the bus offers more—emergency food and clothing, health care, and counseling.

Night Ministry also helps operate a network of youth shelters throughout the city. These include a South Side shelter for females, an emergency shelter for children of adolescent mothers, and a youth emergency shelter for pregnant and parenting adolescents that operates inside a battered women's shelter.

But their most visible presence is on the streets. A worker in a clerical collar goes walking among the prostitutes, the drug addicts, the lost-looking souls. He goes looking for them. And once they get to know him, they go looking for him.

Legal aid groups can help answer a number of questions on a variety of topics. What rights do I have as a young person? Must I return to a foster home? What are the consequences of an illegal act I performed? These legal clinics, usually staffed by young lawyers doing pro bono (charity) work, can take care of simple problems or steer a young person to someone else who can be of immediate help.

Police departments can provide help to some runaways. A police station, since it serves the entire community, must have knowledge of that community. Police will dispense information about agencies and services that exist within their service areas.

Many churches and community organizations sponsor shelters and meal programs for runaways and other homeless people.

Hospitals discourage people who enter with minor illnesses or ailments. Instead of taking care of such people themselves, they refer them to clinics or other sources of help. However, they will not turn away anyone with a major illness or medical need.

Free food centers distribute government surplus milk, cheese, bread, and other essentials. Usually, they are parts of a larger net of services provided by a social service agency. Local grapevines make these services well-known to many runaways. The lines at these centers on food giveaway days are often long.

Churches provide anything from food to surplus clothing to informal counseling. Many serve a semiregular clientele of community residents, but nearly all of them are willing to help a stranger.

Drop-in centers may offer anything from quick advice to a meal and a place to stay. These are usually located in larger cities.

Drug abuse clinics give counseling and sometimes medical services to people with substance abuse problems. Just as important, they work to steer others clear of drugs.

Other agencies are more specialized. The Gay Community Service Center in Hollywood serves young people who want to, but cannot, tell their parents of their sexual preferences. Many of the would-be runaways it serves will run anyway. Others will "come out" to their parents. Even so, they may still run if they meet with disapproval.

No single solution is possible for the diverse runaway population. Runaways have certain things in common, but there are also specific problems that need specific solutions.

The girl who flees sexual abuse at home has different needs from the youngster who left because of an argument with parents. A youth who voluntarily leaves the house with a few dollars to seek his or her fortune has opportunities not available to a neighbor who was kicked out of the house and cannot return. The teenager who escapes a bad foster home has a different set of concerns.

Not all runaways use all of these services. The type of social service used depends on the circumstances that caused the young person to leave home. Although social service agencies work hard to serve runaways and other youth, the results are often less than ideal. Agencies of all kinds serve only a small part of the runaway population. The ones that are served are often served for only one problem (such as drugs or pregnancy), even though many of the runaways are multiproblem cases. Many social workers do not see the problems of runaways as a special case; they are often treated as just another type of delinquent. Services rendered to a runaway may be brief and not followed up. They cure the immediate ache, but not the problem.

WHO AGENCIES HELP

Immigrants, youths who voluntarily leave home looking for adventure or fortune, tend to use free food and services more than other runaways. Since they leave home by choice and not pressure, they often take time to study available services. While others leave home on the spur of the moment, immigrants often have saved money for their departure. They are often less desperate than their counterparts.

Rebels, those who left home because of fights or discipline problems, tend to use the services the least. Their distrust of adults extends to even those who try to give support.

Victims, those affected by physical or sexual abuse, often need immediate help. They populate the women's shelters and are the most likely youthful occupants of hospitals.

Exiles, the throwaways or pushouts, have no choice in their homeless situation. Since they have nothing to lose by contacting police or social agencies (there is no threat to send them back home), they gladly go to anyone who might help.

Refugees, those on the run from foster homes or other institutions, also are wary of many agencies. They, next to victims, have the most to lose by a return "home." Refugees may talk with social workers, perhaps because they have previous experience with them.

Fugitives, those escaping the law, generally keep low profiles. They may use specialized programs, such as drug-abuse clinics. But they obviously want to draw as little attention to themselves as possible.

Many runaways are aware of the problems involved with social service agencies. More than half of the young people in one survey found no agency to be either helpful or appealing.

The agencies do what they can. But the situation of many runaways is very difficult. They cannot return home, they are too old to be adopted, yet they are too young to live on their own.

Not all youths will be helped. But the results for these agencies may be worth the effort. Michele Kipke of Children's Hospital in Los Angeles commented, "Either they get connected with services quickly or they get connected with other hardened kids."

ALTERNATIVE SCHOOLS

Schooling is often the last thing on the mind of a young person who heads for the streets or the road. Academic or social failure in school might be the reason they decided to run.

Alternative schools provide an answer for some troubled students. Most lack the formality of traditional public or parochial schools. Class sizes are much smaller than in regular schools. Classes may be tailored to an individual student's needs.

Orion Center in Seattle is one of those schools. Although funded by the Seattle public school system, this alternative school is part of YouthCare, a Seattle runaway and homeless youth agency. At any given time, there may be about twenty-five students in the school. The year's enrollment totals about 300 students. Two full-time teachers and several volunteers give the one-on-one education some young people need.

"We develop the basic skills—math, English, a little literature, writing," commented YouthCare director Paul Sullivan. "But we also do classes for credit that other schools might consider extracurricular activities. These include classes such as drug education and AIDS education. We also have unique programs. One of them is a partnership with the Center for Wooden Boats. Our students help restore boats. While doing this, they learn math, drawing, and other skills."

The Orion school has two major aims. For some kids, it provides a chance to catch up with their classmates and get back into a regular school. For others, it may be used to prepare for the GED (high school equivalency) examination.

The students get something else out of the alternative school—a heavy dose of self-esteem. Often, this has been an ingredient largely missing in their lives. "It's a very important component in a person's education," said Sullivan. "Once kids develop self-esteem, their test scores increase dramatically."

One particular group aided by the school was young prostitutes. A recent study examined 114 adolescent prostitutes. They were separated into three groups: those who attended Orion, those unable to attend, and those who refused to attend. Four variables were examined: frequency of prostitution, level of depression, level of self-esteem, and attitude toward schools.

The Orion students studied basic academic courses, computer literacy, life skills, and GED preparation. While the others showed improvement over time only in self-esteem, the Orion students improved significantly in all four areas. Their self-esteem climbed, depression dropped, and they had a better attitude toward school. Perhaps most important, the more time they spent in the school, the less time they spent working the streets.

Failure in school is a big reason many run away. Instead of running, consider an alternative program instead. The students here are participating in Vision Quest, a program for young people at risk for being sent to juvenile detention.

5

GOING HOME

I never miss my mom and dad. They're part of my
past now, the way I'd look at it.
—A Seattle runaway

Some runaways make an absolute break with their previous lives. Their parents no longer appear in their daily thoughts, and former friends are as irrelevant as last year's newspaper. School? That's a topic to be forgotten. Maybe it already is forgotten.

But for others, a time may come when the open road loses its magic. Their new life seems as stale and unfulfilling as their old life was. The streets are made of danger, not gold. Poverty, hunger, rootlessness, and exploitation prove to be terrible traveling companions. In short, it's time to go home.

Sometimes a runaway may show up at the doorstep, ring the bell, and be met by grateful mother, father, sister, brother, and dog. All is forgiven, and life goes on with a happy family. This scene is the exception, not the rule.

The alcoholic mother, the abusive stepfather, the intolerant school, the gangs, the pregnancy—these problems are not going to disappear just because a runaway returns home.

To be a successful runaway, a person must erase the past completely. All issues must be forgotten or ignored. This is extremely difficult, especially for young people. Unless these issues are resolved, the runaway will still have thoughts of home.

Most runaways stay away for just a few days and then
return home. Some long-term runaways return home to a
loving family that is willing to work out its problems, but
most will never come back for good.

Even though many runaways leave for the first time at an early age, most still consider their family of origin "home." Every now and then, homesickness strikes. The good times back home remain in their minds. The bad times, for a while anyway, are forgotten.

During these moments, the runaway's thoughts may go something like this: Maybe things weren't so bad after all. Maybe I was being a little foolish. Maybe things will work themselves out. How is my little brother doing? Maybe I can get my job back. At these times, the runaway decides to return home.

Most runaways stay out for three days or less. They sleep over with friends or other family members. These short-term runners have no intention of wandering to the outside world. Instead, they seek a cooling-off period. The girl who sasses her parents or the boy who runs off in a huff still consider themselves part of their families. They stay out long enough to "teach their parents a lesson" or "save face" by avoiding the embarassment of giving in immediately to their parents' wishes.

Theresa left a New Jersey suburb for New York City. After two days, she figured out that the runaway life was not what she wanted. She phoned her worried parents, then returned to a joyful reunion.

Youthful runners respond to their experiences in different ways. Some use them as useful guideposts to future decisions. Others ignore them.

The most likely place to find a runaway is with a nearby friend or relative. The welcome can wear out after a week or so, however, and the runaway must either return home or move on.

One who gained insight the hard way was Patti, another New Jersey native. She left because "my parents didn't understand me." She hitchhiked with a friend to Fort Lauderdale, Florida, where they partied for several days. Patti met Gary, who claimed to be a college student. It seemed like true love. Then Gary and his friends raped her, beat her up, and left her inside a parked car. Patti returned home, sobered by her terrifying lesson. "Maybe I understand myself better," she said.

T.J., from suburban Chicago, also went home voluntarily. He took drugs by day and partied by night. He lived under a bridge, in friends' cars, behind a bowling alley, or with whoever would host him. Then he returned to his mother.

"Some parts of me think that I needed the lesson," he admitted later. "I wasn't too functional then, because of drugs, but [the time away from home] made me a little more respectful for having a place to live instead of hanging out on the streets."

Those who feel they cannot return sometimes encourage those who can to revisit their families. "I can't believe some of the kids in here," said one Los Angeles runaway shelter resident. "I don't understand these little girls who ran away from home because they got spanked or something. What do they expect to find that's better than what they already have? I've seen so many of them. They're 13 or 14 and they take a bus into Hollywood and they either get into drugs and prostitution or they get smart and lucky—and they go back home before they get killed."

Holidays often bring runaways home, at least for a while. They see the Christmas decorations in all of the stores. They hear the carols. They remember the fun and the gifts under the Christmas tree. Why not go home for the holidays and give the family another chance? These runners reunite with their families for Christmas. But if problems at home are not resolved, they may be gone again before the New Year.

Parents, too, may have trouble handling a returning runaway. When the young person fled, both might have blamed the runaway. Then they might have blamed each other. Then they blamed themselves. But when the runaway comes home, he or she might return to being the scapegoat.

Many runaways are afraid to return home. They are ashamed of the lives they have led. Some may not attempt a return because they know they are not wanted. One survey of runaways showed that only 47 percent thought they would be welcome if they went home.

Others come back involuntarily. Police or youth agencies return them to their home and parents against their will. One survey asked, "If you went home, what would you do?" One quarter of those responding said they would run away again.

A youth on the run may be indecisive. Part of the person may wish to rejoin the family, while another part may reject the idea. A middle-class Los

WHAT PARENTS SHOULD EXPECT

The young person calling on the phone or walking through the door will not be the same boy or girl who left a few days or months ago. Parents should keep a few thoughts in mind while anticipating a child's return.

• Be realistic about possible outcomes, and be prepared to cope with the worst. Runaways are easy targets for criminals, drug dealers, and pimps. The child may have been a victim.

• Be willing to consider counseling for themselves and the family. Figure out why the youth left home. Get a counselor or other neutral third party to defuse the situation.

• Prepare for the first contact with the runaway by pre-planning statements. If a parent's statement is negative, the young person might not call again. But if the parent's response shows understanding, the child might return.

• Don't expect immediate results. Even if a parent says exactly the right thing, the runaway might not yet be ready for a return. Communications lines should be kept open, but the young person should not be pressured. At least two or three phone calls may be needed.

• The returned youth might seem like a stranger, harder and more cynical than before. At first, the parent may be seen as the enemy, someone mainly interested in destroying the young person's freedom. The parents may be perceived to be in an unholy alliance with the police, schools, and courts against the recently returned runaway.

• At first there may be a "honeymoon" period. Both parents and youths may be a little too friendly and too kind with each other. This may end suddenly with a temper explosion by parent or child.

• Sometimes the runaway episode can be the spark a family needs. The crisis caused by a family problem may cause members to work together to solve that problem. If the problem is not addressed, then the young person is almost certain to run away again.

• Not all stories have happy endings. Sometimes parents and children are not able to live together. If not, both sides should look into alternative living arrangements for the young person. A child living in an agreeable situation away from the family is preferable to a dysfunctional family in which everyone suffers.

Angeles runaway named Green called her mother weekly. "Each time I tell her I'd be home in a week, even though I know it's untrue," she said. Green's calls will not continue forever. One day, instead of calling, she will show up unannounced at her mother's doorstep. Otherwise, the telephone calls will become less frequent, and eventually they will cease.

Home sometimes seems good compared with the present surroundings. Marie, who spent a year in a foster home, rejoined her family. "I really didn't like it there," she commented. "They didn't let me do anything. I figured that if someone was going to scream at me, it might as well be my mother."

Some runaways return home and stay there. Occasionally they may visit their former streetmates. "What's beautiful is someone who's gotten off the streets and comes back bringing food or whatever, telling others how to get off the street," said Rev. Lee Lowrey of the Night Ministry.

EASING THE TRANSITION

It is not always easy for a runaway to go back and live with his or her parents. A reunion implies that runaway or parents or both made mistakes. Stubborness and lack of communication by parents or children lead to most flights. Absence alone might not make these factors disappear.

No two cases are exactly the same. But some basic situations do occur in the cases of all returns.

There are always worries, on both sides. The runaway may wonder, will there be accusations? Will they understand now what they did not understand before? Parents may overreact to their children. They may start throwing blame immediately or insisting that the young person come home right away.

Returning home isn't easy—the problems that led to running away in the first place don't go away. Family counseling can help get parents and teenagers to communicate with each other.

The runaway's first telephone call home is a major event. It indicates, if nothing else, that the runaway still thinks of his or her family. It also says, although sometimes not well, that he or she still loves them.

That first call probably indicates that there will be more. However, it could be the last. It may take all of the missing youth's nerve just to make the call. Anger and shouts from the parents may reinforce the youth's fears that the parents do not want him or her. It may be months before the runaway calls again, if another call is ever made.

Instead, parents should tell runaways they love them, miss them, and want them back. They should let the runaways know they are genuinely trying to understand their problems. "Say all those gushy things that make people vulnerable but that essentially tie them together," suggested social worker Carol Tweedy.

After one or more phone calls comes the first meeting. The runaway may not go straight home. Instead, he or she may agree to visit the parents on neutral grounds. The first meeting may not solve all problems. It may not solve any problems. If anything, it should be a chance for the family to renew its friendship.

Parents may be able to initiate a runaway's return. Geoff's mother and father invited several of his friends over for a chat. Seven showed up. The parents convinced the friends that they wanted Geoff to come home.

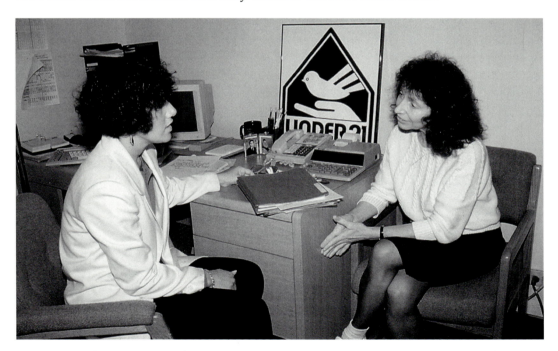

Just coming home may not be enough to hold a family together. For a successful reunion to occur, both the runaway and his or her family need to make some compromises. The objective advice of a counselor can often help parents better understand their children.

WHAT RUNAWAYS SHOULD EXPECT

One major question haunts runaways, particularly those gone a long time. How have my parents changed? How are they going to react to me? There is no simple answer. Every runaway situation is unique. No two parents are alike.

The first telephone call home will be an emotional experience on all sides. For the runaway, it may take all the nerve he or she has to make the call. But this call could be frightening for the parents as well. They may not be prepared to hear from their son or daughter. They may accidentally say some thoughtless thing. If the runaway wants a reunion, he or she should try again, no matter what the results of a first call.

A runaway returning home should not set expectations too high. What most runaways can expect is nothing. It would be nice if his or her parents evolved into people who stopped screaming, stopped beating, stopped molesting, stopped holding expectations that were too high. But that probably will not happen.

This does not mean that the runaway's leaving has not affected the family. Parents might have had a number of reactions. There could be fear, anger, denial, shame, or disbelief. Some might feel intense grief or rejection. Others might feel relief that a source of their problems has gone. Almost all will feel some kind of disorganization.

In some cases, the family situation may be worse than when the runaway left. Many runaways flee home at the beginning of a family breakdown. By the time a runaway decides to give the family another try, it may have already disintegrated.

The best hope for most runaways is that their parents agree to counseling. This may help them realize how their actions and attitudes harm their children. Family counseling may help both parents and runaways communicate with each other for the first time in years.

"I laid it out straight," said Geoff's father. "I said [we] did not understand what the problem was. That didn't mean we thought there wasn't any—we just couldn't identify it. I asked the kids if they heard from Geoff or could contact him, please give him that message. His mother and I wanted things straightened out."

About two weeks later, they got a call. Geoff said he wanted to go home. His parents sent him bus fare, and he came back a few days later.

Michael's parents also had a successful reunion with their son. They kept calm when he called. They asked only where he was and if he wanted to come home. When Michael did return, they asked no questions. At first, he kept to himself in his room. But when he came down from the room, he was ready to talk. The family agreed to counseling, and all made compromises that helped keep the family together.

Even if the runaway moves back home, the crisis may not be over. Some reunited families agree to family counseling in an attempt to resolve their differences. But when the appointment time comes, the family is nowhere to be seen. Some of these families believe that because the runaway has returned, the crisis is over. Others look upon family counseling as a sign of weakness.

One return home does not prevent future runs. Theresa, who rejoined her mother in a tearful reunion, took off again two weeks later. Her mother wanted everything to go smoothly. But she refused to recognize or change the problems that had chased Theresa from the home earlier.

Albert's father was less than overjoyed when police found his son and brought him home. When the cops left, the father started slapping and beating him. Albert ran off again. This time, he made sure not to be caught.

IF YOU CAN'T GO HOME AGAIN

Storybooks usually have happy endings. Reality often provides a much sadder story. Once on the streets for a long time, a runaway rarely goes home. Of those street kids seeking assistance, fewer than half have prospects of returning to their parents.

In Los Angeles, only 20 percent of youth on the run were considered candidates for a return to their families. One recent government report there stated that 60 percent of the youth in runaway shelters did not intend to return to their original living situation. In New York, that number is even less than 10 percent. One survey showed that 35 percent of youth on the streets no longer knew where their parents could be contacted.

Even if a parent is contacted, there is no guarantee of a happy return. Jed Emerson, former director of San Francisco's Larkin Street Youth Center, said that 68 percent of the parents he contacted through his program responded by saying, "You keep the kid."

Todd was ousted from his home during one of his father's rare sober moments. The father simply told him to "move on." He contacted a local priest. The priest talked to Todd's father and mother at their home.

"The father was one of the most unfeeling individuals I have ever encountered—and I meet a broad spectrum," the priest remarked. "He wasn't angry, just cold. He showed absolutely no emotion when he said he didn't want the boy back. 'Let someone else take care of him'—those were his exact words. The mother? Well, she didn't say anything at all, just kind of huddled in a corner. I think there might have been a problem with wife-beating, too."

Not every runaway comes home and stays there. Many find that their bad family situation hasn't gotten any better and take off again. Some want to return but can't locate their families—and sometimes their families don't want them.

Todd did not return home. The priest said, "Legal guardians can be forced to accept a child, but a court can't order parents to love a child. Living in that home would have been emotionally damaging as well as physically dangerous for Todd."

Johnny, a former runaway, commented, "When a kid runs from home, there is usually a gap in the family. But as time passes, the gap closes. So you're no longer the same person. They wouldn't want you back again."

Often, the parental situation that caused the flight remains unchanged. Carol, whose stepfather raped her, returned several months later. Her mother refused to believed that the stepfather had attacked Carol. She sided with the stepfather. Carol left again. This time she did not return.

A boy or girl who stays away from home for more than a week rarely comes back unchanged. Sometimes the parents cannot accept the changes in the runaway. Sometimes the runaway's changes make home life unacceptable.

How the runaway's parents react to a homecoming may depend on the situation. A victim's parent may understand the child's reason for leaving. In the case of a mother, she might have been a victim of the same man. Parents of exiles, who were all but thrown out, might be resentful of seeing the child again. A rebel's parents most likely felt their child was out of control. The child had to change, although the parents did not feel they had to change their own behavior. Fugitives' parents might have disliked their son or daughter's behavior, but they feared punishment the authorities might give. Lower-class immigrants' parents may feel their child is old enough to fend for him- or herself. An upper-class immigrant's parent may dismiss the run as a "phase" a child goes through.

Likewise, what a runaway may expect could depend on the situation that caused the run. Unless a victim's parents received successful counseling, he or she could expect more of the same abuse upon return. Most social workers hesitate to return victims to their homes. Rebels and their families may be able to live together if they get family counseling. However, either or both sides often reject such counseling. Fugitives may end up repeating the problems. For them, counseling may be needed to prevent criminal careers. Immigrants are more likely to be competent runaways, but may return home for economic reasons. Refugees escaping institutions have no desire to return to them. Exiles cannot return.

The runaway's future life depends upon whether he or she decides to go home. That decision rests on a number of factors: the runaway's street smarts, basic nature, emotional stability, and extent to which he or she is angry with the parents.

A young wanderer may return to home wiser than when he or she left. That returnee could be appreciative of home's comforts and wary of the outside world's perils.

Those are the lucky ones. Many return home emotionally scarred, bitter, and cynical. They are no longer children but world-weary adults in young people's bodies.

Some never return.

ADDITIONAL RESOURCES

Hundreds of runaway shelters, switchboards, crash pads, drop-in centers, food giveaway locations, churches, and government agencies are willing and able to help young people away from home. All offer confidential services that can be used by runaways.

The following list is a short one, containing only one or two listings for each metropolitan area. These are not the only sources of help in these cities. But if they cannot help the runaway, they can lead him or her to other organizations that can be of immediate help.

RUNAWAY SWITCHBOARDS
National Runaway Switchboard 800-621-4000
Nineline 800-999-9999
Runaway Hotline 512-463-1980

RUNAWAY SHELTERS AND AGENCIES
Anchorage: Covenant House Alaska 907-272-1255
Atlanta: The Bridge 404-792-1700
Baltimore: Fellowship of Light 410-837-8155
Boston: Bridge over Troubled Waters 617-423-9675
Chicago: Night Ministry 312-935-3366
Cincinnati: New Life Youth Service 513-221-3350
Cleveland: Youth Out Reach Center 216-881-1004
Dallas: YMCA Casa Shelter 214-358-4504
Denver: Runaway Alternative Network 303-698-2302
Detroit: Counterpart Runaway Shelter 313-563-5005
El Paso: Runaway Center of El Paso 915-562-4765
Fort Lauderdale: Covenant House Florida 305-561-5559
Honolulu: Hale Kipa 808-955-2248
Houston: Covenant House Texas 713-523-6904
Indianapolis: Stopover, Inc. 317-635-9301
Kansas City: Restart, Inc. 816-472-5664
Las Vegas: Catholic Community Services 702-385-2662
Los Angeles: Children of the Night 818-908-4474
                 Options: 213-467-8466
Memphis: Family Link 901-725-6911
Miami: Miami Bridge 305-635-8953
Milwaukee: Pathfinders for Runaways 414-271-1560
Minneapolis: Bridge for Runaway Youth 612-377-8800
Newark: Family Violence Program 201-484-4446

New Orleans: Covenant House New Orleans 504-584-1111
New York: Covenant House New York 212-603-0300
Philadelphia: Voyage House 215-545-2910
Phoenix: Tumbleweed 602-271-9849
Pittsburgh: Light of Life Ministries 412-321-4716
Portland (OR): Outside-In 503-223-4121
San Antonio: Youth Alternatives, Inc. 210-340-8077
San Diego: Youth Development, International 619-292-5683
San Francisco: Huckleberry House 415-252-2950
Seattle: Orion 206-622-5555
St. Louis: Shelter the Children 314-351-8306
St. Paul: St. Paul Youth Service Bureau 612-771-1301
Tucson: Open Inn, Inc. 602-323-0200
Washington, D.C.:   American Youth Work Center 202-785-0764
                   National Network of Runaway and Youth Services
                   202-783-7949

FOR FURTHER READING

Artenstein, Jeffery. *Runaways: In Their Own Words: Kids Talk About Living on the Streets.* New York: A Tom Doherty Associates Book, 1990.

Brenton, Myron. *The Runaways: Children, Husbands, Wives, and Parents.* Boston: Little, Brown, 1978.

Elkind, David. *All Grown Up and No Place to Go.* Reading, MA: Addison-Wesley, 1984.

Hyde, Margaret O. *My Friend Wants to Run Away.* New York: McGraw-Hill, 1979.

Hyde, Margaret O. and Lawrence E. Hyde. *Missing Children.* New York: Franklin Watts,1985.

Kolodny, Robert C., Nancy J. Kolodny, Dr. Thomas Bradner, and Cheryl Deep. *How to Survive Your Adolescent's Adolescence.* Boston: Little, Brown, 1984.

Kosof, Anna. *Runaways.* New York: Franklin Watts, 1977.

Madison, Arnold. *Runaway Teens: An American Tragedy.* New York: Lodestar Books (E.P. Dutton), 1977.

Miller, Dorothy, Donald Miller, Fred Hoffman, and Robert Duggan. *Runaways—Illegal Aliens in Their Own Land.* New York: Praeger Publishers, 1980.

Weisberg, D. Kelly. *Children of the Night: A Study of Adolescent Prostitution.* Lexington, MA: Lexington Books, 1985.

GLOSSARY

Chicken. An underage male prostitute. A **chicken hawk** is a customer who pays for sex with the chicken.

Crash. Sleep for free or at an inexpensive price. Runaways may crash with friends, relatives, at crash pads, runaway shelters, or locations provided by religious or social service groups.

Crash pad. A center designed to provide overnight shelter and short-term assistance to a runaway or young homeless person.

Dumpster-dive. Search for food discarded in trash containers, usually behind restaurants.

Exile. A youth who leaves home because of parental rejection. An exile may be a pushout or throwaway.

Exploratory stage. The period in which runaways have overcome their initial fears and begin to learn about the challenges and dangers of their new environment.

Fugitive. A runaway who flees home to avoid the consequences of his or her own behavior. The fugitive leaves to avoid arrest or punishment, but may maintain periodic contact with the home.

Homeless youth. A person under 18 years of age who is in need of services and without a place of shelter where he or she receives regular supervision and care.

Hustling. Any illegal activity undertaken for gain. The word is used particularly to indicate prostitution.

Immigrant. An independent runaway who seeks adventure and freedom. Immigrants do not leave home because of conflicts with parents. The parents, however, may understand or even encourage the child's run. Immigrants comprise only a small percentage of the runaway population.

John. The customer of a prostitute.

Learning disability. A disorder that makes it difficult for a person to speak, read, write, reason, or think.

Neglect. Failure of a parent to provide basic needs of a minor, such as food, shelter, clothing, or medical care.

Physical abuse. The act of a parent, guardian, or parent figure beating, mistreating, or threatening a minor with physical harm.

Pimp. The business manager of a prostitute. The pimp supposedly provides protection for the prostitute, in return for part of the prostitute's earnings. In truth, pimps often virtually enslave both male and female prostitutes, sometimes taking the prostitute's entire earnings and using beatings or torture to prevent the prostitute's leaving.

Pushout. A young person who has been forced out of his or her home by a parent or guardian.

Rebel. A runaway who left home after long-standing hassles with parents. The rebel uses the run as a ploy to get his or her way. Rebels want to live at home, but by their own rules.

Refugee. A young person without a family who leaves a foster home or institution. Refugees run for reasons other than the consequences of their own behavior. They no longer depend on their parents and they feel they have no one for support.

Routinization stage. The period after a runaway has mastered his or her new environment. Once the basics of existence have been conquered, the runaway settles into a routine, and becomes an example for more recent runaways.

Runaway. A person under 18 years of age who leaves home at least overnight without the knowledge or permission of his or her parent or guardian.

Sexual abuse. The act of a parent, guardian, or parent figure involved in rape, incest, sexual physical contact, or threat of sexual contact with a minor.

Spainging. Begging for spare change.

Squat. An abandoned building occupied by runaways and other homeless teenagers.

Survival sex. Sexual acts that are performed for money, shelter, or material favors rather than for affection with the partner.

Throwaway. A young person no longer wanted in the home by the parent or guardian. The throwaway may or may not be forced out of the home (see pushout). But the parents or guardians reject any attempt by friends, relatives, or authorities to have the child returned to them.

Unsettling stage. The initial period of a runaway's time on the street or road. The runaway has not yet secured the necessities (shelter, food) or mastered basic runaway survival skills.

Victim. A young person who runs from physical or sexual abuse inflicted by parents or other family members. Victims fear, yet depend on, parents for support. If that support is dropped, they become helpless vagabonds.

INDEX

A

abandoned children, 22-23
AIDS (acquired immune deficiency syndrome), 40
alcohol abuse, 38-39
arrests of runaways, 41-42, 59

B

Behrens, Tom, 75
bisexual youth, 8-9

C

Chicago, 7-8, 24, 75
child pornography, 54
communications problems, 21-22
confidence games, 59-60
counseling, 84, 87, 88, 90
courts, 43, 44
Covenant House (runaway shelter), 66, 70-72
    Nineline (switchboard) operated by, 73-74
crash pads, 74
crime, 45-46
cults, 46-48

D

deaths of runaways, 48-49
    murders, 72
    of prostitutes, 56
depression, 13, 27, 40
divorce, 17
drop-in centers, 76
drug abuse, 8, 38-40
drug abuse clinics, 76
drug dealing, 56-58
dumpster-diving, 59

E

education
    alternative schools for, 78-79
    as barrier to employment, 61
employment, 60-63

F

families
    abusive, 15-16
    communications problems in, 21-22
    contacts with, 44
    disintegration of, 17
    inability to return to, 88-90
    returning to, 81-88
    of runaways, staying with, 30-31
    street families, 36-38
family counseling, 90
food
    dumpster-diving for, 59
    free food centers for, 76
    at shelters, 66
Fort Lauderdale, 24, 70
foster homes, 17
    running to family of origin from, 30-31

G

Gay Community Service Center (Hollywood), 76-77
gay youth, 8-9, 18, 76-77
girls
    pregnancy of, 18
    as runaways, 12, 13
    sexual abuse of, 15
    shelters used by, 68
Greenhouse (runaway shelter), 66

H

Haight-Ashbury (San Francisco), 11-12
hanging out, 33-35
health, 11-12, 40-41
hippies, 11-12
homosexuality, 8-9, 18, 76-77
hospitals, 76
hotlines, 72-74, 91
Houston, 72
Huckleberry House (runaway shelter), 65, 66

I

incest, 15, 52

L

Lake View (Chicago), 7-8
laws, 10. 41-43
legal aid groups, 75
Los Angeles, 24, 33, 52, 70, 88
Love, Brian, 17, 69
Lowrey, Lee, 9, 36, 52, 85

M

male prostitution, 8-9, 52, 54-56
medical care, at shelters, 66
mental illness, 40-41
murders, 56, 72

N

National Runaway Switchboard, 73
New York City, 24, 33, 52, 70-72, 88
Night Ministry (runaway shelter), 69, 75
Nineline (runaway switchboard), 73-74

O

Operation Peace of Mind (runaway switch-board), 73
Options House (runaway shelter), 66
Orion Center, 78-79

P

panhandling, 60
parents
    children in foster care running away to, 30-31
    children pushed out by, 22-23
    divorce of, 17
    of friends, 29-30
    laws favoring, 42
    permissive, 20
    sexual and physical abuse by, 15-16
    strict, 19-20
pimps, 52-54
police, 75, 83
pornography, 54
pregnancy, 18, 39-40
prostitution and prostitutes, 8-9, 15, 46, 51-56
    shelters and, 68
pushouts, 22-23

R

rape, 15, 53
    of males, 54
Ritter, Bruce, 39, 52, 70, 71
Runaway and Homeless Youth Act (U.S., 1974), 66, 73
Runaway Hotline, 73

S

San Francisco, 11-12, 24
schools, 45
    alternative schools, 78-79
    potential problems in, 27
    as reason for running away, 18-19
Seattle, 24
sexual abuse, 15-16, 52
    women's shelters for victims of, 74
sexually transmitted diseases, 40
shelter (housing), 29-33
    crash pads for, 74
    at runaway shelters, 66
shelters (agencies), 65-70, 91-92
    age of runaways in, 12
    Covenant House, 70-72
    medical care of runaways in, 41
    Night Ministry, 75
    profile of runaways in, 13
    women's, 74
shoplifting, 58-59
social service agencies, 74-78, 91-92
    referrals from switchboards to, 73
suicides, 48

T

telephone hotlines, 72-74, 91
theft, 58-59
throwaway children, 22-23, 57, 73
Travelers Aid Society, 74

V

violence
    against runaways, 9, 33, 46
    as cause of running away, 15-16
    linked to prostitution, 56
    murders, 72
    rape, 53, 54